Microcomputers in Early Childhood Education

Special Aspects of Education

A series of books edited by Roy Evans, Roehampton Institute, London, U.K.

Volume 1
DISADVANTAGED POST-ADOLESCENTS
Approaches to Education and Rehabilitation
Reuven Kohen-Raz

Volume 2
ISRAELIS IN INSTITUTIONS
Studies in Child Placement, Practice and Policy
Eliezer D. Jaffe

Volume 3
PARENTAL PARTICIPATION IN CHILDREN'S DEVELOPMENT
AND EDUCATION
Sheila Wolfendale

Volume 4
EDUCATION FROM THE MULTI-LEVEL PERSPECTIVE
Models, Methodology and Empirical Findings
Edited by Hans Oosthock and Pieter van den Eeden

Volume 5
CLASSROOM COMPOSITION AND PUPIL ACHIEVEMENT
A study of the Effect of Ability-Based Classes
Yehezkel Dar and Nura Resh

Volume 6
CHILDREN'S PLAY
Research Development and Practical Applications
Edited by Peter K. Smith

Volume 7
RISK FACTORS IN INFANCY
Edited by Alice Sterling Honig

Volume 8
PLAY, LANGUAGE AND SOCIALISATION
Perspectives on Adult Roles
Edited by Sue Burroughs and Roy Evans

Volume 9
MICROCOMPUTERS IN EARLY CHILDHOOD EDUCATION
Edited by John T. Pardeck and John W. Murphy

This book is part of a series. The publishers will accept continuation orders which may be cancelled at any time and which provide for automatic billing and shipping of each title in the series upon publication. Please write for details.

Microcomputers in Early Childhood Education

Edited by

JOHN T. PARDECK
Southeast Missouri State University, USA

and

JOHN W. MURPHY
University of Miami, USA

GORDON AND BREACH SCIENCE PUBLISHERS
New York London Paris Montreux Tokyo Melbourne

Gordon and Breach Science Publishers

Post Office Box 786
Cooper Station
New York, New York 10276
United States of America

Private Bag 8
Camberwell
Victoria 3124
Australia

Post Office Box 197
London WC2E 9PX
England

3–14–9 Okubo
Shinjuku-ku, Tokyo
Japan

58, rue Lhomond
75005 Paris
France

Post Office Box 161
1820 Montreux 2
Switzerland

The articles published in this book first appeared in *Early Child Development and Care*, Volume 25, Numbers 2 and 3, Volume 28, Number 2, and Volume 32, Numbers 1–4.

The article 'The Technological World-View and the Responsible Use of Computers in the Classroom' first appeared in *Journal of Education*, Volume 167, Number 2, 1985 © Trustees of Boston University. Reprinted with permission.

Library of Congress Cataloging-in-Publication Data

Microcomputers in early childhood education/(edited by) John T. Pardeck, John W. Murphy.
    p. cm. -- (Special aspects of education, ISSN 0731-8413 : v. 9)
    Includes index.
    ISBN 0-677-21900-8 (pbk.)
    1. Education, Preschool--Data processing. 2. Early childhood education--Data processing. 3. Children and computers.
I. Pardeck, John T. II. Murphy, John W. III. Series.
LB1140.35.C64M53 1988
372'.21'0285--dc19
    88-24429
    CIP

Contents

Introduction to the Series   ix
    Roy Evans

1. Introduction: Microcomputers in Early Childhood Education   1
    John T. Pardeck and John W. Murphy

2. Microworlds, Mother Teaching Behavior and Concept
    Formation in the Very Young Child   11
    Daniel Shade and J. Allen Watson

3. A Developmental Study of Children's Computer-Aptitude
    and Knowledge About Computer Technology   29
    Barbara Burns and Elizabeth Ferguson

4. Assessing Microcomputer Competencies for the Elementary
    Teacher: An Indepth Study of Illinois Schools   45
    Robert C. Morris and Eugene Meyer

5. Young Children's Interaction With a Microcomputer   63
    Steven B. Silvern, Peter A. Williamson and Terry M. Countermine

6. Using the Computer for Early Childhood Screening, Writing
    Objectives, and Developing Local Norms/Records   77
    Carol Mardell-Czudnowski and Dorothea Goldenburg

7. The DAISEY Data System: A Computerized System to
    Support Longitudinal Research   85
    Garrett K. Mandeville, Gail I. Raymond and Lorin W. Anderson

8. Computers and Cognitive Development: A Preliminary
    Statement   97
    John W. Murphy and John T. Pardeck

9. A Critical Look at Children and Microcomputers: Some
    Phenomenological Observations   107
    Larry W. Kreuger, Howard Karger and Kathy Barwick

10. Computer Use With Young Children: Present Perspectives
    and Future Possibilities   121
    Philip B. Waldrop

11. The Technological World-View and the Responsible
Use of Computers in the Classroom   131
John W. Murphy and John T. Pardeck

Index   145

For
Jean, Jonathan, Jamie
and
Karen

Introduction to the Series

Increasingly in the last 10 to 15 years the published literature within the field of care education has become more specialised and focussed: an inevitable consequence of the information explosion and the wider scope of theoretical and practical knowledge being required of students in both the traditional and developing areas of professional training. Students within initial and post-initial training evidently need to have ready access to specialised theoretical and pedagogical resources relevant to the context of their future professional involvements which also develop special aspects of an area of study in a critically evaluative way.

In the study of education and pedagogy, and analytical and experimental approaches of psychology, philosophy, sociology, social anthropology, etc., have provided insights into teaching and learning, into schooling and education. Historically these disciplines have focussed their attention on relatively homogeneous populations. Increased worldwide mobility has created a need for a more pluralistic approach to education — particularly in Western countries — and a more broadly based concern for educational issues related in particular contexts. Hence, futher literature has developed in recent years which is concerned with the pedagogical and curricular issues raised, for example, in connection with the "urban school", minority ethnic groups, disadvantaged and handicapped groups, and children who live apart from their families.

What is frequently missing from discipline-orientated studies is a real appreciation of context beyond the "general". What is often not present in the contextual study is an interdisciplinary analysis of the issue that provides a framework for practice.

The present series — "Special Aspects of Education" — is intended to bridge the gap between the problems of practice, as perceived in a variety of contexts, and theory, as derived from a variety of disciplines.

Books accepted or commissioned for inclusion in the series will manifestly be expected to acknowledge the interdisciplinary nature of the issues and problems in the field of education and care and, addressing themselves to particular contexts, to provide a conceptual framework for identifying and meeting special educational needs.

Roy Evans

CHAPTER 1

Introduction: Microcomputers in Early Childhood Education

JOHN T. PARDECK
Southeast Missouri State University
and
JOHN W. MURPHY
University of Miami

THE SO-CALLED Computer Age is now upon us and is influencing nearly every aspect of modern life. There is little to suggest that the proliferation of computer technology is going to abate; in fact, it appears highly probable that there will be dramatic advances in microcomputer technology in the near future (Pardeck, 1988). All fields of study have begun to adopt the new microcomputer technologies now available. Most of the current uses for computers in the field of education have been aimed at increasing the effectiveness of teachers and administrators, and to facilitate the learning process for students.

Presently, the influence of computer technology is not well understood. That is, educators do not have a clear picture of how microcomputer technology effects the learning process and what the long term consequences will be for students who experience the computerized classroom. In this collection of papers, an effort is made to explore issues related to microcomputer technology; these are 1) to analyze the potential uses of microcomputer technology in early childhood education; 2) to present current research and theory building focusing on microcomputers and early childhood eduction; and 3) to explore critical unanswered questions about microcomputer technology in the classroom. It should become clear from reading the articles in this book that computers have tremendous potential to improve education, as well as the capacity to do great harm if important issues related to this technology are not explored.

Clearly, the educational experience of young children may be improved through the use of microcomputers. Even though much of the early resistance to microcomputer usage by young children emphasized their inability to perform the complex tasks needed to interact with a computer, recent advances in software and hardware suggest that this argument is now moot. Touch screens, voice input devices, and concept keyboards have been developed that allow even two year olds to operate a microcomputer.

The right software and hardware allow young children to do a variety of educational activities. Microcomputers can be effective in teaching reading readiness skills. This technology can also help children learn shape recognition, improve visual discrimination, learn basic arithmetic, improve spelling, and develop story building skills. Cuffaro (1985) has pointed out that the microcomputer can, in particular, help the disabled child have an expanded access to the physical and social world.

Cuffaro (1985) argues that microcomputers can also raise the consciousness level of many teachers, with respect to analyzing the learning process. That is, as teachers consider the influence that the computer has on the acquisition of knowledge, they are pushed to develop greater insights into the learning process and the implications of this activity for children. Clearly, the microcomputer has had a number of important influences on early childhood education.

WHAT CAN MICROCOMPUTERS DO?

Robert Taylor, in his edited book, *The Computer in the School* (1980), suggests that the microcomputer might play three potential roles in the learning process: 1) it can serve as a tutor; 2) it serves as a potential tool; and 3) it can be programmed to function as a tutee. It would appear obvious how the microcomputer can serve as a tutor for basic learning activities. For example, the microcomputer can be used as an instrument for teaching young children basic mathematics, spelling, or grammar. John Seely Brown notes that the microcomputer can be used to teach subtraction and higher level mathematical functions (Dreyfus and Dreyfus, 1985). What is particularly noteworthy about the microcomputer is that is provides instant feedback to students which helps them to learn mathematical skills more rapidly than other methods. Additionally, the microcomputer can be used as a word-processor, a useful tool for even young children, as well as a medium to learn new geometrical shapes and designs.

Seymour Papert (1980) is a pioneering figure in the development of strategies for using the microcomputer as a tutee. Through the introduction of a new language, known as LOGO, Papert has attempted to illustrate ways that children can learn rational thinking for programming, and at the same time develop an appreciation for geometry and logic by actually creating geometrical and logical relationships.

From a traditional educational viewpoint, there is little reason to sneer when the microcomputer is used as a teaching machine. The microcomputer can be easily programmed to teach basic arithmetic and spelling rules (Papert, 1980, p. 36). In fact, Papert is probably correct when he states:

"The idea of the computer as an instrument for drill and practice...appeals to teachers because it resembles traditional teaching methods (and) also appeals to the engineers who design computer systems. Drill and practice applications are predictable, simple to describe, efficient in use of the machine's resources."

But obviously, the question should be raised whether this is the kind of tutoring or training that modern education wishes to emphasize. It must be noted, however, in areas of training that are rule-like, the microcomputer can probably be successfully used. Since the microcomputer can do the job of teaching rote memory faster and with less pain than older teaching methods, such advancements should be praised. The critical question, however, is since the computer appears to be a powerful tool for teaching basic educational skills, should educators move beyond this drill-and-practice stage? This, no doubt, is where the debate begins on the role of the computer in early childhood education.

Since Papert (1980) argues that the computer can be used effectively as a tutee, a number of critical issues must be considered that relate to how he views the learning process and his theory of how the mind works. Papert suggests that the mind resembles a computer. Specifically, he builds his theory on Piaget's work and refers to it as an "epistemological" approach to understanding the mind. Papert views the mind to be an information-processing mechanism, and refers to this thesis as "cognitivism." The microcomputer, in Papert's view, is an idea machine that operates on the cognitivist's model of thinking. Papert concludes that children can master this way of thinking by actually programming a computer, and thus through this process bring their inherent ability to fruition. Papert (1980, p. 27) writes:

"I have invented ways to take educational advantage of the opportunities to master the art of deliberately thinking like a computer, according, for example, to the stereotype of a computer program that proceeds in a step-by-step, literal, mechanical fashion...What is most important in this is that through these experiences, these children would be serving their apprenticeships as epistemologists, that is to say learning to think articulately about thinking."

Papert suggests that the implementation of his cognitivist framework in the classroom, through the use of a microcomputer, would transform our understanding of ourselves and of society. Since the stakes are high, Papert's revolutionary ideas about thinking and the learning process must be critically examined. In fact, the argument could be made that the real importance of Papert's position is that educators will be pushed to examine his theory closely, before adopting the microcomputer as an intricate part of the classroom experience. Indeed, if this critical examination is not conducted, the implications are great for students of all ages and for the larger society.

UNANSWERED QUESTIONS

The key issue related to the eventual success of computerized instruction is information. Can knowledge be transformed into "bits" of information, categorized and placed within the memory of a computer, and regulated by step-wise instructions without dire consequences? Writers such as Herbert and Stuart Dreyfus (1986) claim that information is unduly formalized, and thus misconstrued by digitalization. On the other hand, Allen Newell, Herbert Simon, and Robert Wilensky, argue that this is not the case (Rose, 1984). Somewhere in between are a host of researchers who recognize that computerization has not advanced as rapidly as originally expected. Marvin Minsky, one of the first persons to study artificial intelligence, believes that progress has been inhibited because of the inability of computers to handle "common sense" knowledge (Dreyfus and Dreyfus, 1988). In other words, many computer experts are beginning to recognize that daily life is very complex and reality may be interpreted in a variety of ways. Their point is that computerization does not fare well in such a complicated setting.

Take Papert's work on LOGO as an example. Due to Piaget's influence, Papert adopted a structuralist view of cognition. This is the strategy that has been followed by most computer theorists and programmers. Hence language is assumed to be comprised of elementary parts, which are linked together by fixed laws (Newmeyer, 1986). When speech is conceived in this way, the likelihood of programming language is thought to be good. After all, if computers are going to interact successfully with humans, the issue of language is certainly important. Nonetheless, Terry Winograd (1984) has concluded recently that computerization destroys the interpretive side of language. This is quite an admission on his part, for his program SHRDLU was thought to present a significant breakthrough in natural language programming. The crux of the problem is whether language is merely a system that can be dissected and reassembled without any loss of meaning.

Why is a structuralist rendition of language compatible with programming requirements? Simply put, ambiguous data cannot be tolerated by a computer (Johnson, 1986). Only input that can be defined explicitly and easily classified can be adapted to computer use. Moreover, irregular routines are very difficult to program. Portrayed as a matrix of structures, language can be manipulated and made to conform to the demands of computerization. Yet is language an inanimate object? Many philosophers, social scientists, and critics of computers say no (Murphy and Pardeck, 1986). Their objection is that language is not static, but is always expanding. And following shifts in interpretation, a person's reality is significantly altered. As suggested by Winograd (1984), language resists computerization, because speech acts do not have exact boundaries. Therefore, at this stage in the development of software and hardware, language use is seriously misrepresented by computerization. Interpretation and thus dynamism are treated as irrelevant or, at least, ancillary to communicative competence.

In response to this untenable situation, Roger Schank (1977) and his collaborators at Yale are attempting to introduce "scripts" into their research on artificial intelligence. These stories include the rules and other information persons use daily to make sense of their environment, including the behavior of other community members. As might be suspected, this effort has not been successful. The reason for this failure is quite simple: any script that is used must be stereotypical. Consequently, knowledge is placed within an idealized framework. Most important for education, however, is that users of computers are confronted by a strange mode of representing knowledge. In order to operate a computer successfully, children must assume that information can be analyzed without regard for situational exigencies. Contextless knowledge must be accepted as legitimate.

Accordingly, Margaret Boden (1977) writes that computers are not simply tools, but manipulators of symbols. This area of symbol manipulation is where many unanticipated problems may arise, when computers are applied to classroom use. Research has illustrated that the presence of computers may change the organization of a classroom, yet overlooked is how this technology may affect the cognition of children (Murphy, 1986). Teachers must remember that unique, and possibly problematic, imagery is conveyed to students by computers. Due to the emphasis that is placed on precision, for example, student's beliefs about facts, thinking, and learning may be adversely altered. Creativity may be stifled, along with the ability to think critically. As alluded to by Papert, students may begin to assess and respond to events in a mechanistic manner.

What does all this talk about structuralism, scripts, and language use mean? Specifically, research needs to be undertaken by educators in the areas that are currently the focus of attention for computer experts. The impact of the theoretical and conceptual constructs presupposed by computerization must be understood. While computers are instructing students, more than facts may be presented. Students may be introduced to a portrayal of reality that has little relevance, but may be inappropriate for education in the long-run. Furthermore, when students are young they are unlikely to approach critically their first encounters with computers. Unless educators are aware of how computers may influence both the physical and cognitive environments in the classroom, education may be unproductive. Computers, in short, must be treated as an agent that intervenes actively in the educational process.

OVERVIEW OF THE CHAPTERS

Shade reports fascinating findings on computer competencies of 2 and 3 year old children. Shade's research challenges the notion that only children in the concrete stage of development can master the microcomputer. Suggested by his research is that even very young children, who are in the preoperational stage, can develop basic computer skills. He concludes that the computer microworld has tremendous potential for improving the learning process for even very young children and is only limited by imagination.

Burns' and Ferguson's article explores the computer-aptitude and the microcomputer knowledge level exhibited by young children. The Morris and Meyer study also focuses on microcomputer competencies; however, they analyze how administrators and teachers view these competencies in their students. Burns' and Ferguson's research demonstrates that little discernible differences can be found between kindergarten and third-grade children in terms of computer aptitude, literacy, and interest in the microcomputer. Given Shade's findings concerning the computer competency levels of children in the preoperational stage of development, the findings by Burns and Ferguson are not surprising. Burns and Ferguson introduce a rather intriguing idea pertaining to why computer aptitude and knowledge about computer technology are similar in the kindergarten and third grade groups. They suggest that peer interaction may be the best explanation for similarity between these groups. In other words, children teaching children through peer interaction may well provide a better explanation for how children become computer literate then cognitive development theories.

Morris and Meyer conclude that administrators and teachers see a dramatic increase in the computerization of classrooms at all grade levels. No doubt this finding is not particularly unexpected. The respondents in their research, however, felt that students in lower grades (K-4th) understand less about microcomputer functions than those in higher grades (5th and 6th). The research by Burns and Ferguson would appear to challenge this notion, since they conclude that computer aptitude and literacy are not necessarily issues related to grade level or cognitive development. Clearly, more research needs to be conducted pertaining to these contradictory findings.

The paper by Silvern, Williamson and Countermine reports the findings of a qualitative study, designed to explore how children interact naturally with a microcomputer. They conclude that natural play is an extremely effective approach for introducing children to microcomputer technology. Even though the authors point out the methodological flaws of their study with refreshing candor, a number of useful questions are raised concerning computer literacy that need to be addressed in future studies.

The Mardell-Czudnowski and Goldenberg article is very short and highly specific. They introduce the DIAL-R (Developmental Indicator for the Assessment of Learning-Revised) screening test.

The DIAL-R is a computer-based program that provides an accurate assessment of a range of factors related to success in school. The program provides feedback for administrators, teachers, and parents on suggested learning objectives for children in the following three areas: 1) motor ability, 2) conceptual acuity, and 3) language use. The DIAL-R program stores up to 200 children's scores and allows administrators in particular to analyze class, school, or district scores and develop norms for a given school district. The Mardell-Czudnowski and Goldenberg article offers new ways for school districts to generate important screening information through computer technology.

Mandeville, Raymond, and Anderson focus on the use of computers in collecting test data on children and measuring student performance. These processes are discussed with respect to the DAISEY Data Capture System (DDCS) used in the South Carolina public school system. The authors argue that the DDCS has important implications for research on child development, specifically for evaluating preschool intervention programs.

Murphy and Pardeck rely on advances in contemporary European philosophy and offer a preliminary statement on the impact of computers on cognition. They argue that the centerpiece of computerization is technical or instrumental rationality. Accordingly, a style of cognition referred to as naive realism must be adopted by those who expect to operate successfully a computer. Associated with cognitive theory is a belief in an objective reality, which the mind must mimic if valid knowledge is ever to be acquired. Papert's structuralism, for example, is a rendition of realism. Obviously, a particular view of education accompanies realism. Through interaction with a microcomputer, children are subtly socialized. Suggested by Murphy and Pardeck is that the development of a particular, and problematic, personality syndrome may be encouraged through computerization.

While adopting a phenomenological perspective, Kreuger, Karger, and Barwick contend that a child's *"Lebenswelt"*, or "life-world," is violated by the theoretical tenets that sustain computerization. In other words, the interpretive significance of everyday existence is dismissed as unimportant, or, maybe more damaging, is portrayed as an impediment to the discovery of factual information. These writers illustrate how a child's conception of space, time, and social relations may be distorted as a consequence of interacting regularly with a computer. Moreover, play is transformed into a technical exercise, devoid of moral and ethical considerations. While Papert may find this sort of mechanistic cognition intriguing to analyze, Kreuger, Karger, and Barwick suggest that students trained to think in this manner would be socially inept. Consistent with phenomenology, they believe that reality is thoroughly interpretive and thus socially constructed. Therefore, failure to appreciate the complexity of social existence will result in students achieving only a minimal level of communicative competence.

Waldrop provides an excellent survey of the issues most germain to the use of computers by young children. Most important, however, is his suggestion that no technique can promote learning. This position is very important to remember, for many persons tend to believe that society can be improved simply as a result of technical innovation. The Computer Age appears to be organized on the basis of this theme. On the contrary, however, technological advancements may be unrelated to upgrading the quality of education provided by a school system. Without a general educational philosophy, a master plan for implementation, and a comprehensive program of research, very little may be accomplished through the use of microcomputers. Educators should not become enamored of technique to the extent that these crucial factors are overlooked. Waldrop's message, stated simply, is that technical issues are not necessarily central to the successful use of computers in the classroom or elsewhere.

And finally, Murphy and Pardeck describe in some detail the computer "micro-world," which is currently the focus of attention of many computer theorists. First, the theoretical character of this domain is discussed, while second, the practical implications of this world-view for education are assessed. Once students enter the computer micro-world, their experience of reality may be immediately imploded. A device that is supposed to expand a student's horizons may have the opposite effect. Many computer experts, accordingly, argue that computers will not contribute significantly to the generation or dissemination of knowledge, until programs are invented that can accomodate more than empirical or quantitative data. An attempt has been made to computerize belief systems, yet this research has not been overly successful (Colby, 1973). Nonetheless, Murphy and Pardeck maintain that unless the traditional components of the computer micro-world are expanded, computer technology may eviscerate a child's education. Because education is a *social* activity, the way information is presented by computers must become socially sensitive.

In sum, the aim of this volume is to provide both an empirical and theoretical discussion of the impact of computer technology on education. Little research has been done in either area. Nonetheless, the trend is to place students in front of a microcomputer as early as possible, in order to insure that they become technically competent. Given the situation, educators must become aware of how computers influence the physical and cognitive environments in the classroom. It is hoped that this book will facilitate that process.

References

Boden, M. (1977). *Artificial Intelligence and Natural Man*. New York: Basic Books.

Colby, K.M. (1973). Simulations and Belief Systems. In R.C. Shank and K.M. Colby (eds), *Computer Models of Thought and Language* (pp. 251–286). San Francisco: W.H. Freeman

Cuffaro, H. (1985). Microcomputers in education: why is earlier better? In D. Sloan (ed), *The Computer in Education* (pp. 21-30). New York: Teachers College Press.

Dreyfus, D. and Dreyfus, S. (1988). Making a mind versus modeling the brain: artificial intelligence back at a branchpoint. *Daedalus*, **117**(1), 15–43.

Dreyfus, H. and Dreyfus, S. (1986) *Mind Over Machine*. New York: The Free Press.

Dreyfus, H. and Dreyfus, S. (1985). Putting computers in their place: analysis versus intuition in the classroom. In D. Sloan (Ed). *The Computer in Education: A Critical Perspective* (pp. 40–63). New York: Teachers College Press.

Johnson, G. (1986). *Machinery of the Mind*. New York: Time Books.

Murphy, J. (1986). Humamizing the use of technology in education: a re-examination. *International Review of Education*, **32**(2), 137–148.

Murphy, J. and Pardeck, J. (1986). Technologically mediated therapy: a critique. *Social Casework*, **67**(10), 605–612.

Newmeyer, F. (1986). *The Politics of Linguistics*. Chicago: University of Chicago Press.

Papert, S. (1980). *Mindstorms: Children, Computers, and Powerful Ideas*. New York: Basic Books.

Pardeck, J. (1988). Micro computer technology in private social work practice: an analysis of ethical issues. *Journal of Independent Social Work*, **2**(1), 71–81.

Rose, F. (1984). *Into the Heart of the Mind: An American Quest for Artificial Intelligence*. New York: Harper and Row.

Schank, R. (1977). *Scripts, Plans, and Understanding: An Inquiry Into Human Knowledge Structures*. Hillsdale, NJ: L. Erlbaum.

Taylor, R. (ed) (1980). *The Computer in the School: Tutor, Tool, Tutee*. New York: Teachers College Press.

Winograd, T. (1984). Computer software for working with language. *Scientific American* **251**(3), 131–145.

CHAPTER 2

Microworlds, mother teaching behavior and concept formation in the very young child

DANIEL D. SHADE
Southeast Missouri State University
and
J. ALLEN WATSON
University of North Carolina at Greensboro

Forty-one preschool children, 21 two-year-olds and 20 three-year-olds, and their mothers were randomly assigned to two treatment groups: A microworld designed to teach the concept on inside/outside via item sorting on screen and a computer experience designed to drill the alphabet. Daily videotapes of mother/child dyads were coded and scored using a revision of the Wood and Middleton (1975) Assisted Problem Solving Scale (r = .80). A sorting task patterned after the microworld followed treatment. Microworld mothers teaching strategies differed significantly from alphabet mothers with software type affecting dyad interaction. A 2×2 ANOVA yielded no significant main effects for group or age on the post-test. However, the age/group interaction approached significance ($p = .053$) with three-year-olds in the microworld group correctly sorting more objects. A repeated measure mixed model ANOVA revealed a highly significant within-group effect; three-year-olds within the microworld group were significantly more successful in correct item sorting on a daily basis.

KEY WORDS: Preschool, microcomputers, microworlds, drill-and-practice, mother/child interaction.

PRESENT controversy over the microcomputer's monster/messiah characteristics (Shepard, 1985), premature conclusions that preschool children should not work with computers (Barnes and Hill, 1983; Bass, 1985; Brady and Hill, 1984; Cuffaro, 1984; Tan, 1985; Sprigle and Schaefer, 1984; Zajonc, 1984), recent re-evaluation of the preschool child's cognitive abilities (Gelman and Baillargeon, 1983; Papert, 1980; Watson, Nida, and Shade; 1986), and questions about how mothers will teach their young children to use a microcomputer led to the research reported in this article.

A goal central to our research was to provide additional data in the hope of resolving the controversy as to whether or not preschool children should work with microcomputers. In spite of the observational, anecdotal nature of much of the current research involving young children and microcomputers (Brady & Hill, 1984), it is possible to draw some tentative conclusions about the accessibility of computers to young children. It has been established that preschoolers can work with standard keyboards and other parts of the microcomputer configuration (Borgh and Dickson, 1983; Muller, 1983; Rosen, 1982; Shade, Nida, Lipinski, and Watson, 1986; Swigger and Campbell, 1981; Watt, 1982). Several well-designed observational studies (Perlmutter in Butler, 1985; Lipinski, Nida, Shade, and Watson, 1986; Shade, Nida, Lipinski, and Watson, 1986) have reported some or all of the following: preschool children turned the microcomputer on and off, removed and replaced diskettes properly, followed the instructions of a 4-choice picture menu, changed programs (disks) as often as three times in a ten-minute period, worked at the computer together in naturally occurring dyads (peer interaction), spent a great deal of their time talking about the computer activity, and exhibited mostly prosocial behaviors (turn-taking, helping, sharing). Limited work in this area has been done with children under three years of age, however Dickson (Reed, 1983) and diRenzo (1983) have shown that children 18 to 24 months can master a portion of the above cited computer operating skills. We intended to refine our knowledge-base concerning microcomputer accessibility to very young children.

A second goal central to our research was to provide empirical evidence that even very young, preoperational children could benefit from cognitive exercises using a two-dimensional computer screen (Barnes and Hill, 1983; Brady and Hill, 1984; Cuffaro, 1984; Watson et al., 1986; Zajonc, 1984). Barnes and Hill (1983) began the controversy with a statement that children "must reach the stage of concrete operations before they are ready to work with microcomputers (p. 11)." The primary point voiced by critics was that young children could not cognitively manipulate abstract stimuli to learn from computer instruction. Most of the critics assumed a rigid, abrupt view of cognitive stage transition. Gelman and Baillargeon (1983) conducted an extensive review of the research related to Piagetian stage theory. Citing numerous research studies they concluded that under certain conditions, young preschool children behave in a non-egocentric manner, ignore misleading perceptual cues, integrate information about states and transformations, and are capable of deliberate thinking. Barnes and Hill (1983) stated that preoperational children cannot classify, yet research shows that young children can classify objects taxonomically (Mervis and Crisafi, 1982; Nelson, 1973; Rosch, Mervis, Gay, Boynes-Braem, and Johnson, 1979; Ross, 1980) depending on the level of stimuli they are shown: basic rather than superordinate or subordinate (Sugarman, 1979). Watson, *et al.* (1986) reviewed young child/computer literature and found that neither recent cognitive theory nor research data supported the "concrete stage only" viewpoint.

The final goal of our research was to investigate mother/child interactions in the context of microcomputer instruction. Wood and Middleton (1975) have shown that mother, because of her general knowledge and relationship with her child, usually knows the best level at which to intervene in a teaching situation. Wood and Middleton also noted that mother often intervenes to help the child by taking over one or more operations. By doing so, she frees the child to concentrate all his/her attention and effort upon a more narrow range of alternatives within the task. Wood and Middleton called this the "region of sensitivity to instruction," a borderline between what the child is currently capable of doing and what s/he cannot (also Vygotsky, 1978, concept called "zone of proximal development"). We predicted mothers would concentrate their attention upon appropriate instructional intervention and would vary their level of involvement with regard to the type of software they used (discovery oriented versus drill-and-practice).

Since we had some assurance that young children were capable of operating the computer, able to sort on the basic level, and work best with mother, we chose to program a computer microworld as a vehicle for mothers to teach their children to sort objects that belong either inside or outside a house. Papert (1980) described a microworld as a construct of reality, a simulated environment where children have direct access to a particular concept or concepts and the operational ability to manipulate those concepts in meaningful ways. Our research questions were as follows: Can very young children (20 to 36 months) learn to work moderately complex microworld software (four step keyboarding rather than single step)? What strategies do mothers select to teach microcomputer manipulation? Will software differences (microworld versus drill-and-practice) have an effect upon mother's teaching strategies? And finally, is a microworld an effective way to develop concept formation and sorting skills in young children?

METHODS

Subjects

The subjects involved in this study were 46 preschool children enrolled in a university one-hour enrichment program and their mothers. Children attended this program twice a week. While the children explored a Piagetian-based play-school environment, mothers attended a one-hour lecture on various child rearing topics. There were two groups of children; two-year-olds and three-year-olds with mean ages of 2.01 and 2.83 respectively. Of the original 46 children, five did not participate. One child's mother was confined to bed via doctor's orders, vacation plans interfered for another, and three others simply did not care to be involved.

Children were randomly assigned to either the microworld or drill-and-practice group. There were 10 twos and 11 threes in the microworld group and 11 twos and 9 threes in the alphabet group. In terms of gender, there were 11 males and 10 females in the microworld group; while the alphabet group had 12 males and 8 females. The families for both groups were intact. Parents were highly educated; nearly all of them had a bachelors degree or equivalent. A full third of the mothers had masters degrees and half of the fathers had either a masters or doctorate.

Design

The study utilized a Post-test Only Control Group design (Campbell and Stanley, 1963) with some repeated measures (see variables below). The subjects were not randomly selected although randomly assigned to groups. All daily sessions with mother and child interacting together at the microcomputer were videotaped from closed circuit cameras and observed from behind two-way glass.

Variables

Independent variables The independent variables of interest were: treatment group (experimental vs. control), age-of-child (two vs. three), and software type (microworld vs. drill-and-practice).

Dependent variables Numerous dependent measures were recorded for each dyad. The first was the total daily number of objects correctly sorted inside or outside the graphic house as displayed on the computer screen. This variable constituted the repeated measures aspect of the design.

A second dependent variable was measured using an adaption of the Wood and Middleton (1975) Assisted Problem Solving Scale. Four levels of mother teaching strategy or intervention were coded at the end of the study: (1) No intervention, (2) Verbal instruction, (3) Indicates materials (points), and (4) Demonstrates. Frequencies of these levels were coded and recorded for each mother.

A third dependent measure, time mother spent in the "region of sensitivity to instruction (Wood and Middleton, 1975)," was determined in the following manner. Any intervention level at which a child's success rate fell below 50% (Wood and Middleton, 1975) was earmarked as that child's "region" of sensitivity. Once the region was established it became a simple matter to count the number of interventions mother made at that level or higher (a mother who demonstrates has taken over more steps of the operation than a mother who verbally instructs).

Additional daily dependent measures were obtained including: time at the computer, mother directed success, child directed success, and success resulting from each of the four intervention levels. Success was defined as the ability to make the software do what it was intended to do and was measured as successful keyboard strokes. The difference between mother directed and child directed success was locus of control as indicated by verbal statements of intent.

The post-test was administered at the conclusion of the final 15-minute session. Children played a game where they could place real objects inside or outside a three-dimensional copy of the microworld software display. A "blind" experimenter recorded the total correct sorts for each child.

Pilot Study

A pilot study was performed to assess a similar population's knowledge of the inside/outside concept and their familiarity with the objects that were utilized in the microworld group. The pilot study was performed on an equivalent group of 23 preschool children. Children were shown 35 different objects and asked if the object belonged inside or outside a house. It was concluded that children between 18 and 24 months did not know the concept since they consistently placed all the objects either inside or outside. Between 24 and 36 months children generally knew the correct classification for 1 to 3 items. Between 36 and 42 months children sorted 90% (about 31 items) correctly. Ten familiar objects (children could label), five inside and five outside, that were consistently incorrectly sorted were chosen and incorporated into the microworld software.

Treatment

The experimental group interacted with specially developed software (using SpriteLogo for the Apple IIe) centered around the concept inside-outside. Treatment consisted of four 15-minute sessions. Children, sitting in their mother's lap, worked at an Apple IIe with dual-disk, Amdex color monitor, and SpriteLogo interface card. The screen background, drawn by the turtle, contained the cut-a-way of a five room house surrounded by green grass and blue sky. All keys were covered with blank stickers except for the following. Ten keys were covered with pictures of the objects they controlled: five inside objects (TABLE, LAMP, BED, TV, POTTY) and five outside objects (CAR, SWING, SLIDE, FENCE, STOP SIGN). Four additional keys had arrows on them pointing up, down, right, and left. Finally, there was a "stop" and a "go" button. The "go" button caused the software to function by animating the objects. When a child was satisfied with object placement on the screen, he/she could press the "stop" button to fix the object in place, press another object key, press the "go" button, and begin manipulation again. When complete the monitor screen desplayed 10 objects in varied positions in and out of the house.

Children in the control group worked with software designed to drill the alphabet. Pressing any letter key would cause a highly colorful, animated cartoon corresponding to that letter to appear on the screen. Although these children received a computer experience, it was totally different in format and philosophy from the experimental (microworld) group. As such their experience should be thought of as a "placebo" similar to subjects given a sugar tablet in drug studies.

Mothers in both groups received little training on the two types of software other than a brief verbal explanation of how the software operated and a "help" chart that hung on a nearby wall. The help chart contained an abbreviated list of software operation steps. It was hoped, by limiting mother's training, that conditions similar to home could be simulated and ecological validity improved (Bronfenbrenner, 1979).

Reliability Checks

Quite an elaborate setup was required for the coding of data in order to maintain the controls necessary to ensure reliability. Two coders and a third head-coder worked simultaneously. Data coders sat in front of large-screen videotape monitors on opposite sides of the room. Behind a partition and out of sight of the coders sat the head-coder, who was responsible for running the two videotape machines which allowed coders to code two sessions at a time. After every fourth treatment session was coded (approximately 20% of the total interaction time), the head-coder flipped a silent switch which resulted in coders watching the same session. This made it possible for coders to work on different treatment sessions and, without their knowledge, view a single session simultaneously for reliability checks. The coders had headphones which allowed them to listen to the coding tape with one ear and the videotape with the other. Inter-rater reliabilities consistently exceeded .80; ranging from .82 to .86.

Microworld versus drill-and-practice Data analysis revealed that software type (microworld versus drill) influenced how mothers interacted with their children. Sign tests showed that microworld (MW) mothers gave significantly more control over software manipulation to their children between day one (D_1) and day four (D_4). Specifically the following changes in mother intervention strategy for the MW group were noted: (1) No mother intervention increased ($D_1 = 3.38$, $D_4 = 11.43$, $p = .0002$); (2) Mother verbal instruction increased ($D_1 = 16.81$, $D_4 = 36.57$, $p = .0005$); (3) Mother indicates materials decreased ($D_1 = 24.71$, $D_4 = 12.62$, $p = .0266$); (4) Mother demonstrated decreased ($D_1 = 38.52$, $D_4 = 23.71$, $p = .0004$). For the most part, there were no significant changes between consecutive days except for mother verbalizations ($D_1 = 16.81$, $D_2 = 30.14$, $p = .0005$), mother indicates materials ($D_2 = 20.14$, $D_3 = 14.43$, $p = .0015$), and mother demonstrates ($D_1 = 38.52$, $D_2 = 26.95$, $p = .0072$). There were no significant changes for the drill-and-practice (DP) mother's intervention strategies between consecutive days or between day one and day four.

Kendall's Coefficient of Concordance (MW's $W = .58$, $p = .0005$; DP's $W = .55$, $p = .0005$) revealed significant agreement among children in both groups as to which mother intervention strategy produced the most success. However, the rank ordering of child success by intervention level was different for each group. For the MW group rank ordering of the mean ranks was as follows: verbal instruction (3.45), indicates materials (3.17), demonstrates (1.98), and no intervention (1.40). For the DP group they were: verbal instruction (3.28), no intervention (3.15), indicates materials (2.38), and demonstrates (1.20). Kendall's tests were also performed to see if mothers within each group agreed on an overall intervention strategy; this was found to be the case although patterns differed again for each group. In the MW group ($W = .46$, $p = .0004$) the ranking of intervention levels was as follows: demonstrates (3.24), verbal instruction (2.81), indicates materials (2.71), and no intervention (1.24). The DP group mothers ($W = .63$, $p = .0005$) agreed on a different overall pattern: no intervention (3.85), verbal instruction (2.70), demonstrates (1.90), and indicates materials (1.55).

Mothers, in this study, did not spend much time in the region of sensitivity to instruction. As explained earlier, any level in which a child's success rate fell below 50% (Wood & Middleton, 1975) was earmarked the region of sensitivity to instruction. Binomial tests were used to determine this region by noting which levels of intervention each child was significantly successful in and those s/he was not ($p = q = .50$, one-tailed, $p < .05$). The total time each mother spent in the "region" was then calculated and correlated with several child measures of success. For instance, Pearson correlations between the percent of time mother spent in the "region" and the percent of child success was non-significant for the MW and DP groups respectively; $r = .27$, $p = .225$ and $r = .32$, $p = .158$. Furthermore, neither group showed a significant relationship between the time mother spent in the region and the number of mother directed successes ($MWr = .29$, $p = .187$; $DPr = .44$, $p = .052$). We feel confident in our ability to distinguish between mother directed and child directed success. Pearson correlations between child directed success and mother non-intervention were high for both groups ($MWr = .70$, $p = .0005$; $DPr = .98$, $p = .0005$). In addition, we are not concerned with the near significance ($p = .052$) of the correlation between DP mother's time in the "region" and mother directed success as it has already been shown that these mothers were highly inactive. Finally, the time mother spent in the "region" failed to correlate significantly for either group for any of the following measures: total child success resulting from non-intervention, verbalization, indicating materials, and demonstrating.

However, it should be noted that MW mothers were not totally blind to their child's developmental needs. Spearman Rank Correlations between the age-of-child (in months) and mother's use of intervention levels yielded two interesting relationships for this group; (1) the older the child, the more likely was mother to use verbal instruction ($r = .51$, $p = .017$) and (2) the younger the child, the less likely was mother to use non-intervention ($r = -.51$, $p = .018$). No such relationships emerged in the DP group but that makes sense when we focus on the Binomial tests reported earlier. In the MW group (four step keyboard manipulation, $n = 21$) 7 threes (.33) and 1 two (.05) were successful more than 50% of the time. In the DP group (one step keyboard manipulation, $n = 20$) 8 threes (.40) and 4 twos (.20) experienced success more than half the time. Thus we can see that differences in software format influenced mother intervention. The drill-and-practice software, which produces success for any child who can push a key, simply did not require mother's to monitor child success. The microworld software, on the other hand, required mothers to respond differentially based on their child's age.

Experimental versus control   A 2 × 2 ANOVA revealed no significant main effects for group or age on the post-test (sorting task). (However the age-group interaction approached significance ($p. = .053$)

Table 1. Analysis of Variance Summary for Total Objects Classified by Treatment (2) by Age (2)

Source	SS	Df	F	Prob.
Treatment	5.015	1	0.3759	0.544
Age	0.622	1	0.0466	0.830
Treatment Age	53.121	1	3.8920	0.053
Error	493.474	37		

Examination of the cell means by way of simple main effects analysis (Keppel, 1982) revealed that no two means were significantly different at the alpha = .05 level. However, the simple main effect for the three-year-olds by group approached significance.

Table 2. Simple Main Effects of Total Placed for Age = 3 by Treatment (2)

Source	SS	Df	F	Prob.
Between Groups	46.0626	1	3.0069	0.1000
Within Groups	275.7374			

Table 3. Means and Standard Deviations of Total Objects Classified by Treatment (2) by Age (2)

Variable	Mean	SD	n
Microworld	7.3333	3.4400	21
Two's	6.3000	3.7431	10
Three's	8.2727	3.0030	11
ABC Group	6.6500	4.0429	20
Two's	7.8182	3.0271	11
Three's	5.2222	4.8161	9

Visual inspection of these cell means showed that the three-year-olds in the MW group sorted more objects correctly than the three-year-olds in the DP group.

Post hoc power calculations (Keppel, 1982) revealed this near significant difference to be due to the strength of the effect rather than chance. In other words, the lack of statistical significance was due to the moderate number of subjects in each cell.

A mixed model repeated measures ANOVA [A × (B × S)] for the MW group revealed no significant findings for the day-of-week main effect or the age/day interaction. However, a highly significant main effect for age was present.

Table 4. Repeated Measures ANOVA Within-Group Effects of Total Objects Placed for Age (2)

Sources	SS	df	F
Age	492.39058	1	25.61359*
Error	365.25227	19	

*$p < .0005$

Within the MW group, three-year-olds correctly oriented more graphic objects (mean = 7.075; range 6.4 to 7.4) than did the two-year-olds (mean = 2.22; range 1.63 to 3.0) on a daily basis.

DISCUSSION

It is important to clarify that this study was not a comparison of early childhood teaching techniques. It was never our intention to compare the efficacy of microcomputer presentation of concepts to other teaching methods. Our main goal was to set to test the notion of preschoolers as cognitively blind-folded when microcomputers are present. We chose a microworld format for our software because it adhered most closely to the guidelines set by Papert (1980), Lawler (1982b), and others (Watson, Nida & Shade, 1986). In light of these conditions, the following conclusions have been drawn.

Mother's Reactions to Software

Mothers in this study were capable, given the minimal training they received, of teaching their preschool children to use microcomputers; although the overall plan of attack differed for each group. Considering the software differences, somewhat complex to incredibly easy, mother teaching behavior was quite logical. MW mothers paid close attention to their children and adjusted their interventions over the four-day period. MW mother's began intervention by demonstrating and pointing and ended up either verbally instructing or doing nothing at all. Mothers in the DP group had less rigorous software with which to deal and conse-quently did less intervening. They made no change in strategy over time and when they did intervene, which ranked second to doing nothing, they found verbal instruction to be sufficient. These software differences led to the conclusion that mothers in the MW group relinquished more control over software operation to their children as time progressed.

Another software based conclusion concerns mother's apparent lack of sensitivity to her child's "region of sensitivity to instruction (Wood and Middleton, 1975)." It was shown that the time mother spent in the "rigion" was not related to any of the child success measures. Furthermore, the overall agreement on intervention strategy between mothers using the same software (microworld versus drill) does not agree with rank ordering of intervention levels by amount of child success. Children had the most success, regardless of group, when mothers used verbal instruction. Nevertheless, mothers in the MW group exhibited high levels of demonstration throughout. From here the groups were quite different with the second highest rank going to mother indicates (points) for the MW group and no intervention for the DP group. Therefore, it can be concluded that mothers in both groups reacted more to software format than to child behavior cues when choosing an intervention strategy (although mothers in the MW group appeared sensitive to child age).

Age of First Introduction to Computers

In spite of warnings (Barnes & Hill, 1983; Cuffaro, 1984) that "children must reach the stage of concrete operations before they are ready to work with microcomputers," three-year-olds in the MW group were rather successful. They showed the greatest task persistence as evidenced by a moderately high correlation between the age of the child and the total time spent at the computer ($r = .49$, $p = .024$) and the fact that the younger children tended to wander around the room a great deal. Furthermore, they learned to classify or sort significantly better than two-year-olds in the same group ($p = .0005$) and nearly significantly better than three-year-olds in the DP group ($p = .053$). MW two-year olds, on the other hand, sorted no better than children in the control group.

Based upon these findings it can be concluded that age of first introduction to the computer is dependent upon software content and competencies required. Highly colorful, cartoon-like graphics that respond to any key pressed, such as used in the DP group, require little preparation, instruction, or specific computer skills. If children can push a key, they can operate this type of software with a high degree of success. On the other hand, software with the exploration oriented content that requires sequential manipulation of several keys requires particular competencies. Such software demands much of the child both cognitively and physically.

Therefore, from the findings of this study, we contend that age two is an appropriate time to introduce children to the computer simply for the purpose of creating positive attitudes towards technology. Software should be chosen with the goal of providing a pleasant, positive, and non-frustrating experience for the child. Single-key operated software is perfect for this task. It is further recommended that three-years of age be earmarked as the appropriate time for increased computer training and the introduction of discovery-based microworld software. This study showed that children at this age are capable of increased cognitive sophistication and keyboard manipulation.

Microworld Software

Ziajka (1983) predicted that some day we may want to add computer-generated images on a screen as a new form of representation that children evoke and manipulate. Others (Sprigle and Schaefer, 1984; Tan, 1985; Watson et al., 1986) have also concluded that the abstractions inherent in two-dimensional graphic displays would not inhibit learning for young preschool children. Piestrup (1985) noted that microcomputer presentation of material is really no more abstract than picture books (the staple of early childhood education) and far less static. To those who would argue otherwise (Barnes and Hill, 1983; Bass, 1985; Cuffaro, 1984) we add the superior performance of MW three-year-olds over MW two-year-olds and DP three-year-olds in learning the inside/outside concept. Our three-year-olds in the microworld group had little difficulty learning from two-dimensional graphic displays. Of course, two salient features of the microworld software used in this study lie at the foundation of these findings. First, the graphic material presented contained representations of concrete objects which were not far removed from the children's everyday experience. Second, children were given control of object movement and position. These factors together make microworld software a responsive and dynamic experience. Responsive compared to the experience of flipping through a picture-book (Piestrup, 1985) or watching TV (Forman, 1985); dynamic in that children were able to use previously learned information in a new way (Lawler, 1982a, 1982b; Papert, 1980).

The ability to relate the computer experience to previous learning is critical to the formation of microworlds and distinguishes them from other software formats. Papert (1980) stated that microworlds should be "syntonic" or, in other words, adaptive to the social or interpersonal environment. Therefore, a microworld is powerful for a person when it relates and unifies knowledge gained in diverse experiences (Lawler, 1982b). Microworlds are powerful because they contain phenomenon which relate to a child's experience and because they embody the simplest model that an expert can imagine as an acceptable entry point into the world of knowledge (Lawler, 1982a).

What will be the end result of the current emphasis on computer research with young children? Will microworlds replace story books, teachers, blocks, and fingerpaint? We seriously doubt it. Rather we think the microworld will emerge as a powerful educational tool in many aspects similar to the pencil (Papert, 1980). Like the pencil, microworlds demand little and give much. The potential is only limited to one's imagination.

References

Barnes, B.J., and Hill, S. (1983).   Should young children work with microcomputers: Logo before Lego? *The Computing Teacher*, **10**, 11–14.

Bass, J.E. (1985).   The roots of Logo's educational theory: An analysis. *Computers in the Schools*, **2**, 107–16.

Borgh, K., and Dickson, W.P. (1983).   Two preschoolers sharing one microcomputer: How they handle it. *Onwisconsin Computing*, **2**, 6–10.

Brady, E.H., and Hill, S. (1984).   Young children and microcomputers: Research and directions. *Young Children*, **39**, 49–61.

Bronfenbrenner, U. (1979).   *The ecology of human development: Experiments by nature and design*. Cambridge: Harvard University Press.

Butler, P.A. (1985).   Research notes: Social interactions in young children's learning about computers. *Journal of Educational Computing Research*, **1**(3), 363–64.

Campbell, D.T., and Stanley, J.C. (1963).   *Experimental and quasi-experimental designs for research*. Chicago: Rand McNally.

Cuffaro, H.K. (1984).   Microcomputers in education: Why is earlier better? *Teachers College Record*, **85**, 559–68.

Forman, G. (1985).   The value of kinetic print in computer graphics for young children. In W. Damon and E.L. Klein (Eds.), *Children and computers: New directions for child development*, No. 28, San Francisco: Jossey-Bass. Gelman, R., and Baillargeon, R. (1983). A review of some Piagetian concepts. In J.H. Flavell and E.M. Markham (Eds), *Carmichaei's manual of child psychology* (Vol. 3), New York: Wiley.

Lawler, R.W. (1982a, June).   In the lap of the machine. *Boston Review*, 8–10.

Lawler, R.W. (1982b, August). Designing computer-based microworlds. *Byte*, 138–60.

Lipinski, J.M., Nida, R.E., Shade, D.D., and Watson, J.A. (1986).   The effect of microcomputers on young children: An examination of free-play choices, sex differences, and social interactions. *Journal of Educational Computing Research*, **2**(2), 147–68.

Mervis, C.B., and Crisafi, M.A. (1982).   Order of acquisition of subordinate, basic, and superordinate level categories. *Child Development*, **53**, 258–66.

Muller, A. (1983).   Preschoolers at the computers. *Commodore Magazine* **4**(4), 86–88.

Nelson, K. (1973).   Some evidence for the cognitive primacy of categorization and its functional basis. *Merrill-Palmer Quarterly*, **19**, 21–39.

Papert, S. (1980).   *Mindstorms: Children, computers, and powerful ideas*. New York: Basic Books.

Piestrup, A. (1985).   Silicon chips and playdough. In A.M. Gordon and K.W. Brown, *Beginnings and beyond: Foundations in early childhood education*. Albany, NY: Delmar, 399–402.

Reed, S. (1983, March). Preschool computing: What's too young? *Family Computing*, 55–69.

Rosch, E., Mervis, C.B., Gay, W.D., Boynes-Braem, P., and Johnson, D.W. (1976).   Basic objects in natural categories. *Cognitive Psychology*, **8**, 382–439.

Rosen, S. (1982, October).   Texas: Lighting the way via video. *Learning*, 34–36.

Ross, G.S. (1980). Categorization in one- to two-year-olds. *Developmental Psychology*, **16**, 391–96.

Shade, D.D., Nida, R.E., Lipinski, J.M., and Watson, J.A. (1986). Microcomputers and preschoolers: Working together in a class-room setting.
Computers in the Schools, **3**(2), 53–61.

Shepard, N. (1985). Technology essiah or monster. In W.M. Matthews (Ed.),
Monster or messiah? The computers impact on society. Jackson: University Press of
Mississippi.

Sprigle, J.E., and Schaefer, L. (1984). Age, gender, and spatial knowledge
influences on preschooler's computer programming ability. *Early Child
Development and Care*, **14**, 243–50.

Sugarman, S. (1979). *Scheme, order and outcome: The development of classification in
children's early block play*. Unpublished doctoral dissertation. University of
California, Berkeley.

Swigger, K.M., and Campbell, J. (1981, March). *Computers and the nursery school*.
A paper presented at the meeting of the National Educational Computing
Consortium, Denver.

Tan, L.E. (1985). Computers in preschool education. *Early Child Development and
Care*, **19**, 319–36.

Vygotsky, L.S. (1978). *Mind in society: The development of higher psychological
processes*. (M. Cole, V. John-Steiner, S. Scribner, and E. Soubeman, eds.
and Trans.). Cambridge: Harvard University Press.

Watson, J.A., Nida, R.E., and Shade, D.D. (1986). Educational issues concerning young children and microcomputers: Lego with Logo? *Early Child
Development and Care*, **23**, 299–316.

Watt, D. (1982, August). Logo in the schools: Putting Logo in the classroom has
led to some interesting results. *Byte*, 116–134.

Wood, D., and Middleton, D. (1975). A study of assisted problem solving. *British
Journal of Psychology*, **66**, 181–91.

Zajonc, A.G. (1984). Computer pedagogy? Questions concerning the new
educational technology. *Teachers College Record*, **85**, 569–77.

Ziajka, A. (1983). Microcomputers in early childhood education? A first look.
Young Children, **38**, 61–67.

CHAPTER 3

A Developmental Study of Children's Computer-Aptitude and Knowledge About Computer Technology

BARBARA BURNS
Mount Holyoke College
and
ELIZABETH FERGUSON
Mount Holyoke College

A new test of computer-aptitude and knowledge about computer technologies for young children was developed based on the Computer Aptitude, Literacy and Interest Profile (Poplin, Drew and Gable, 1984). The measure of computer-aptitude was based on tests of number estimation, comprehension of directions, and geometric color and form analogies. Young children's knowledge about computer technologies was measured in four subsections: 1) background experience, 2) technical knowledge, 3) awareness of understanding of the role of the computer in society, and 4) perception and understanding of how the computer works. Results from testing kindergarten and third-grade children with equal experience are described and the implications of this type of research for issues in basic and applied developmental psychology are discussed.

KEY WORDS: Computer aptitude, computer literacy, computer knowledge, child development.

THE INCREASING importance of computer-based technologies in the workplace has led to the development of a variety of types of computer-aptitude tests for adults (Schmidt, Gast-Rosenberg and Hunter, 1980). Typically these tests include tasks that are closely tied to programming and, in fact, predict success in computer programming training courses quite well. The Computer Programmer Aptitude Battery (CPAB), for example, includes tasks such as completing a flow chart, translating word descriptions to mathematical notation, estimating answers to fairly complex computations and defining vocabulary words associated with data-processing (Johnson, 1972). More recently the subject population interested in working with computers has expanded to include individuals, such as women and minorities, who have not had the opportunities to develop computer-programming related skills (Brillhart, 1980; Miura and Hess, 1983). Thus, previous types of aptitude tests, developed for a restricted well-defined group of people, are not well suited to identify talented individuals and to document the success of training programs.

The Computer Aptitude, Literacy, Interest Profile (CALIP) was developed to meet these needs (Poplin, Drew, and Gable, 1984). The CALIP employs six subtests with items of a range of difficulty for persons from junior high school to adult ages. The subtests include number estimation, the completion of graphic patterns, reasoning with number, letter and word analogies, interest and motivation, and computer literacy (i.e., knowledge). Norms for these capabilities associated with success in computer courses, have been developed for gender, and age and potentially provide "an empirical basis for administrators, business managers, and teachers to allocate organizational resources" (Poplin, etc., 1984, p. 3).

The primary purpose of the present study was to develop a test for young children based on the CALIP such that children's aptitude for and knowledge about computers could be measured across age.

METHOD

Subjects

Two groups of children participated in this study. In the first group, (n = 13) children were between the ages of five and six years and attended the Gorse Child Study Center at Mount Holyoke College. The second group (n = 14) consisted of children between eight and nine years of age who attended a third-grade public school in South Hadley, MA.

Materials and Procedure

In the present study, the Computer Aptitude, Literacy, and Interest Profile (CALIP) developed by Poplin et al. (1984) was modified and adapted for young children. Our test, which we will refer to as the Children's Computer-Aptitude and Knowledge Test (CCAKT), consists of four subsections: 1. number estimation, 2. direction comprehension, 3. analogical reasoning, and 4. general knowledge about computers.

1. *Number Estimation–K* For the kindergarten children, the number estimation subsection contained five trials which required the child to estimate the number of black squares on a card and five trials which required the child to judge the relative quantity of two rows of squares on a card. The counting cards contained from three to eighteen squares of which the actual number of black squares varied from two to twelve. For the quantity judgment cards, the child was presented with a given card which depicts two rows of equal length; one row has more squares than the other. The child was asked to point to the row which has more squares.

Number Estimation–3rd Grade The third grade children were given 10 cards similar to those contained on the original CALIP (Poplin et al., 1984). These cards contained varying numbers of black and white squares and the children were asked how many black squares were on each card. The number of squares on each card ranged from 45 to 72 and the number of black squares from 24 to 54.

2. *Comprehension of Directions–K* For the kindergarten children, the examination of the comprehension of directions included 12 questions. The task involved the placement of a toy turtle in relation to a large rectangular piece of cardboard. The child was asked to move the turtle in a forward, backward, left, or right direction. Following each question the turtle was returned to its original position by the experimenter.

Comprehension of Directions–3rd Grade The third grade children were simply asked to point in each of the four directions (F,B,L,R).

3. *Analogical Reasoning* The analogical reasoning subsection consisted of 15 questions each of which included three geometrical shapes indicating a common variable: either color or form. The particular analogies chosen were based on the study by Alexander, Willson, White and Fuqua (1985). The child was given a choice of four geometric shapes from which to choose the shape that best completed the series presented. The shapes used included two sizes of a triangle, a circle, and a rectangle. The colors of the shapes used were

red, blue, yellow and green. In the first five questions, color was held constant and the analogy was based on form, on the second five the reverse was true. On the last five trials both color and form were required to successfully complete the series.

4. *Computer Knowledge* The final section of the CCAKT contained an interview which was designed to determine the level of a child's interest and knowledge of computers. The interview questions could be divided into four categories: A) Background in computers, B) Technical knowledge of the computer, C) Awareness of the computer in society, and D) Perception of the computer and how it works. A list of the questions (1–13) is shown in Table 1.

Procedure

The CCAKT was administered to each child individually in two 10 minute sessions. Kindergarten children were interviewed in an adjoining room to their classroom; third grade children were interviewed in an isolated corner in the classroom.

Scoring

For sections 1, 2, and 3 of the CCAKT the percentage of correct responses was taken as the child's score. Section 4 consisted of an interview in which the child answered questions about her knowledge of computers. The system developed to quantify the child's responses was as follows:

4A. *Knowledge of Computers: Child's Background in Computers.* For this subsection, one point was given for a positive answer (e.g., if she had a computer at home) in response to questions 1, 2, and 4. For questions 3 and 5, a child received one point for each different activity mentioned (e.g., "drawing and writing on the computer" would receive a score of two points).

4B. *Knowledge of Computers: Technical Knowledge.* In the technical knowledge section (questions 6 and 7), the categories used to classify the children's levels of knowledge were scored in a hierarchy from perceptual (1 point) to functional (2 points) to relational (3 points). Pure physical descriptions, or perceptual knowledge, consisted of the child merely describing what she sees before her (e.g., "keys are the little buttons"). Functional answers included descriptions of the child's own experience with the computer. A response such as the "The keyboard has buttons you push" would be scored within this category. The most abstract category of technical knowledge consisted of functional answers which showed a knowledge of the causal relationship between the item mentioned (i.e. the keys) and the workings of the computer. We have referred to these answers as "relational" responses. For example, if the child said "When you press the keyboard it shows up on the screen", the response was scored in the relational category.

4C. *Knowledge of Computers: Awareness of the Computer in Society.* For these questions, (8–10), one point was scored for each alternative provided by the child.

4D. *Knowledge of Computers: Perception of the Computer and How it Works.* There were several types of scoring systems devised for questions 11–13. For question 11, is a computer a machine?, one point was given for a positive answer. For question 11a, in which the child was asked to explain what makes the computer a machine, the responses were categorized into one of two groups: a physical description of the machine, or a description of the distinction between a computer and a living thing (i.e., the explanation that the computer is a machine based on a comparison of its abilities and needs to those of a human being).

Responses to question 12, which asked what happens when you push a key, were divided into three categories: perceptual (1 point), perceptual/functional (2 points) and functional (3 points). A perceptual response included what the child sees (e.g., "it makes a line"). The functional response included what the computer does and how it relates to the key pressed (e.g., "you press it and the letter you just pressed goes on the screen"). The perceptual-functional category was used for a response in which a child was not able to verbalize the functional relationship yet that relationship was implied through the child's accompanying hand motions.

Responses to question 13, "How is a computer the same/different from a TV?", were categorized into the three categories of responses as described for question 6 and 7: 1. The responses based on perceptual information in which the child describes the similarities of the physical attributes of each machine (e.g., "they both have screens"), 2. The functional response which refers to a child's comparison of the similarities of each machine's function (e.g., "the TV has shows and the computer draws); and 3. The relational responses in which the child refers to the relation between the machines (e.g., "on a TV you can change channels and on a computer you can change disks").

The responses to question 13 were also categorized according to whether the child gave an active (e.g., "you can write on it (computer), and you can pick your shows (TV)") or passive (e.g., "you can't watch TV on a computer) response concerning what can be done on a computer. Active and passive, therefore, refer to the level of activity indicated in the response.

Results and Discussion

Children's Computer Aptitude (Sections 1,2,3) and Knowledge (Section 4) Profile

1. Number Estimation

The estimation task was analyzed to determine if the kindergarten and third grade scores differed. Both groups scored well (76% correct for kindergarten and 91% for third grade) and there was no significant difference for the age groups ($t(25) = 1·59, p > ·01$).

2. Comprehension of Direction

The ability to comprehend directions was very high for both ages tested (86% for kindergarten and 100% for third grade). There was, however, a significant difference between the two ages in performance ($t(25) = 2·42, p < ·025$).

3. Analogical Reasoning

The analogical reasoning section contained trials in which form, color, or both dimensions were varied in the series of objects to be completed. An analysis of variance revealed a significant effect of age for the overall scores ($F(1,25) = 50·56, p < ·01$); the third grade children performed better than the five year olds (97% correct compared to 77%). A more specific analysis of the analogical reasoning trials revealed an effect of type of trial (color, form, mix) $(F(2,50) = 34\cdot14, p < \cdot01)$. The overall mean percent correct of each trial type was 99% for color, 91% for form, and 71% for mix across both ages. Figure 1 depicts the mean score comparison for each group. Across both ages children performed equally well on the color and form subsections $(q(50) = \cdot08, p < \cdot05)$. For both the color and form subsections, the children's scores were significantly higher than performance on the mix subsection: color versus mix $(q(50) = \cdot28, p < \cdot01)$; form versus mix $(q(50) = \cdot20, p < \cdot01)$.

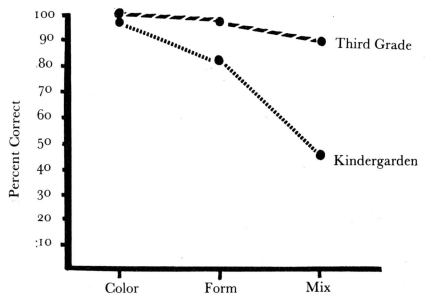

Figure 1.   Mean percent correct for the color, form, and mixed analogies in the analogical reasoning section of the Children's Computer Aptitude and Knowledge Test (CCAKT).

The analysis of variance revealed an interaction of age and subsections (color, form, and mix). Results of this analysis revealed that the performance pattern for the kindergarten children was color $>$ form $>$ mix (color vs. form $- q(25) = \cdot13, p < \cdot05$; color vs. mix $- q(25) = \cdot50, p < \cdot01$; form vs mix $- q(25) = \cdot27, p < \cdot01$). The third graders followed a different pattern in which performance on all three sections did not differ (all p's $< \cdot05$).

When the subsections were compared across age it was found that the kindergarten children and the third graders did not differ on the color subsection $(q(50) = \cdot02, p > \cdot05)$, but for both the form and mix subsections the third grade children performed significantly higher than the kindergarteners (form $- q(50) = \cdot 14$, $p < \cdot 05$; mix $- q(50) = \cdot 45$, $p < \cdot 01$).

4. Knowledge-about-Computers Interview

Table 1 summarizes the answers given in response to the 13-question interview concerning the child's knowledge about computers. The responses from each of the four categories of questions will be considered in turn.

Table 1 Responses from Kindergarten and Third Grade Children to the Computer Knowledge Interview

A. Child's Background in Computers

1. Have you ever used a computer before?

	Yes	No
Kindergarten	13	0
Third Grade	12	2

2. Do you have a computer at home?

	Yes	No
Kindergarten	1	12
Third Grade	5	9

3. What have you done on the computer?

	Games	Drawing	Writing	LOGO
Kindergarten	4	9	1	0
Third Grade	9	1	2	1

4. Do you like working on the computer?

	Yes	No	Sometimes	Never Used
Kindergarten	12	0	1	0
Third Grade	12	0	0	2

5. What do you like about working on the computer?

	Fun	Games	Drawing	Buttons/Keys	Turtle	Easy
Kindergarten	2	1	4	2	1	1
Third Grade	7	3	0	2	0	3

B. Child's Technical Knowledge of Computers

6. What are the keys?

	Physical Description	Child's Experience	Functional	Don't Know
Kindergarten	6	2	1	1
Third Grade	8	1	0	5

7. What is the screen?

	Physical Description	Child's Experience	Functional	Don't Know
Kindergarten	3	3	2	5
Third Grade	4	3	4	3

C. Child's Awareness of the Computer in Society

8. What are computers used for?

	Games	Drawing	Writing	Help Work	Read	Answer Machine	Other
Kindergarten	4	5	10	2	1	0	0
Third Grade	6	1	2	5	0	3	2

9. Where are computers used?

	Work/ Office	Other	Classroom	Computer Store	Home	Don't Know
Kindergarten	2	3	10	2	4	0
Third Grade	10	0	6	0	4	1

10. Who uses computers?

	Self	Friends/ Kids	College Students	Teacher	Family	Business People	All People	Don't Know
Kindergarten	0	2	1	1	3	0	4	3
Third Grade	1	7	2	2	2	8	2	1

D. Child's Perception of the Computer and How it Works

11. Is a computer a machine?

	Yes	No
Kindergaten	13	0
Third Grade	14	0

11a. What makes a computer a machine?

	Physical Description	Lack of Animism	Can't Learn by Self	Don't Know
Third Grade	6	5	2	1

12. What happens when you push a key?

	Perceptual	Perceptual-Functional	Functional	Don't Know
Kindergarten	5	1	5	1
Third Grade	7	0	6	1

13. How is a computer same/different from TV?

	Perceptual	Functional	Relational
Kindergarten	8	8	3
Third Grade	10	11	3

13a.

	Active	Passive
Kindergarten	5	8
Third Grade	7	7

A. Child's Background in Computers. Answers to the first question: "Have you ever used a computer before?" revealed that almost all the children (n = 13, kindergarten; n = 12, third grade) had had previous experience with the computer in some form (see Table 1A question 1). Answers to the second question, "Do you have a computer at home?" revealed that five of the third grade children owned computers and 1 kindergarten child had a computer at her home. The types of previous experience (question 3) varied slightly between the two groups: the kindergarten children were more experienced with drawing on the computer (n = 9) whereas the third grade children had more experience with computer games (n = 9). When asked in question 4 if they liked working with the computer, the replies were overwhelmingly positive in both groups (n = 12, kindergarten; n = 12, third grade).

Question 5 focused on what the children liked about working with the computer. The answers were much less varied for the third graders than for the kindergarteners. The third graders said that it was fun (n = 7), that they liked games (n = 3), or that it was easy to use (n = 3). Some kindergarten children also mentioned fun (n = 2); others responded that they enjoyed drawing (n = 4), using the turtle (n = 1), or playing games (n = 1).

B. Technical Knowledge of the Computer. There was little difference between the two age groups regarding technical knowledge of the computer. When asked what the keys are, (question 6), the majority of the children's descriptions were physical (n = 6, kindergarten; n = 8, third grade). Only 3 children across both ages gave responses from the viewpoint of their own experience. Only 1 child in the kindergarten provided a response which indicated an understanding of the causal relationship between actions on the keys and the effects on the computer (i.e., functional response).

Responses concerning the screen (question 7) were distributed across all three categories with little difference between ages (See Table 1B question 7).

C. Awareness of the Computer in Society. Questions 8, 9 and 10 refer to the children's awareness of computers in the world around them. When asked what computers are used for, (question 8), the kindergarten children focused on writing (10), drawing (5), and games (4). The third-graders' responses centered on games (6), and on the computer being used to help people with their work (5). The responses to question 9 "Where are computers used?", showed an emphasis on the classroom (10) for the kindergarten children (n = 6 for the third grade), and on the office (10) for the third grade children (n = 2 for the kindergarteners). In response to who uses computers (question 10), the children's answers were distributed across a wide range of categories. Although answers from both age groups were quite similar, the third graders generated more ideas overall and included a category of business people (n = 8).

D. Perception of the Computer and How it Works. All 27 children agreed that the computer is a machine (question 11). The kindergarten children were unable to explain why it is a machine, but, in contrast, the eight year olds gave a variety of types of answers. The two predominant categories of responses to this question were physical descriptions of a machine (n = 6) (e.g., "it has wires and a plug), and the descriptions of the computer as a machine due to its lack of animism (n = 5). The third grade children said that the computer was a machine because it had to be taught; it needed a human to make it work. This answer was scored separately as a more complex distinction between inanimate and animate objects.

Questions 12 and 13 focused on the children's perceptions of the computer itself and how it works (See Table 1). Both ages were evenly distributed for perceptual answers (n = 5 for kindergarten, n = 7 for third grade) and functional (n = 5 vs n = 6) in response to question 12. The perceptual-function category was used for the response of one kindergarten child whose answer to "What happens when you push a key?" was "It goes rrrr" accompanied by the child making circles with his finger to indicate the machinery inside.

Question 13 centered on the differences between a computer and a TV. Responses were evenly distributed across the perceptual (n = 8 for kindergarten, n = 10 for third grade) and functional categories (n = 8, n = 11 respectively). In addition, three children from each age group verbalized the similarities in terms of relational properties between the two machines.

Scores for the activity level indicated by child's response to question 13 revealed almost equal numbers of children from each age group in each category: active (n = 5 for kindergarten vs n = 7 for third grade) and passive (n = 8 vs n = 7). Clearly, there were no differences across the two age groups in the children's ideas of the computer in terms of the active-passive dimensions.

As detailed above, the responses to many interview questions could be categorized in terms of perceptual, functional and relational responses. As summarized in Table 2 the number of responses and pattern of responses in each category are highly similar for both age

Table 2   Summary of Perceptual, Functional, and Relational Responses to Questions about the Computer Provided by Kindergarten and Third Grade Children

Interview Question	Category	Age	
		Kindergarten	Third Grade
6	Perceptual	6	8
	Functional	2	1
	Relational	1	0
7	Perceptual	3	4
	Experience	3	3
	Functional	2	4
	Relational	–	–
12	Perceptual	5	7
	Percep.-Func.	1	0
	Functional	5	6
	Relational	–	–
13	Perceptual	8	10
	Functional	8	11
	Relational	3	3

groups. This similarity of patterns of responses certainly reflects a similarity in the kindergarten and third-grade child's understanding of the computer. In other domains of knowledge in which the groups differ in amount of experience, a dominance of perceptual responses by the young children and the emergence of functional and relational responses by the older children would be predicted (see Mandler, 1984 for a review).

Summary Score. Table 3 shows a comparison of the kindergarten and third grade children's score on the interviewbased on the method

Table 3   Composite Score for Section 4. Computer Knowledge

Interview Question	Age	
	Kindergarten	Third Grade
1	1.00	.86
2	.08	.36
3	1.08	1.14
4	1.00	.86
5	.85	1.07
6	1.00	.71
7	1.15	1.57
8	1.77	1.57
9	1.69	1.57
10	1.08	1.79
11	1.00	1.00
11a	—	1.07
12	1.62	1.79
13	2.04	1.71

of scoring described above. An analysis of the mean scores for kindergarten and third grade for the four sections of the interview revealed no effect of age $(F(1,25) = \cdot 84, p > \cdot 05)$, nor a significant interaction between age and the four subsections of the interview $(F(3,75) = \cdot 51, p > \cdot 05)$. The mean scores for kindergarteners and third graders were as follows: Section A—·80, ·86; Section B—1·08, 1,14; Section C—1·15, 1·64; and Section D—1·17, 1·39 for kindergarten and third grade children respectively.

GENERAL DISCUSSION

Our interest in the questions explored in the present work is grounded in two important areas of research: First, the relation between a developing knowledge base and the level of cognitive development, and secondly, the inter-relation of social and cognitive processes across development.

In the present study, kindergarten and third-grade children were tested who had approximately equal levels of experience with the computer. Results from the computer interview generally reflect this shared level of computer knowledge. The particular method of analysis employed in characterizing children's answers revealed no developmental differences in the use of perceptual, functional or relational responses (See Table 2). The pattern of answers to question such as "What are the keys?" and "What happens when you push a key?" was similar for both age groups. This finding is in sharp contrast to much of the developmental literature which characterizes knowledge representation across development as a progression from perceptual to more abstract representation (see Mandler, 1984, for an extensive review).

The present research represents the "tip of the iceberg" in terms of studies of the relation of a developing knowledge base and developmental changes in reasoning (McKeithen, Reitman and Reuter, 1981). More detailed examinations of how children, at a wider range of ages, represent their developing knowledge about computer-based technology and reason with that information is important for the applied study of computers and children's education, as well as for basic research issues on cognitive development. Given the rate with which school systems are implementing computers into the curriculum, the amount of computer experience will soon become much more uniformly correlated with age. Ames and Murray, (1982) underscore this argument by drawing a parallel to research on the effects of television: "relatively little quality work was carried out in the years before everyone had a television set; thus the opportunity to look at relevant control groups and conditions was lost. It is hoped that 10 years from now we will not be in a position of lamenting that the most important research about computers is precluded because nearly every individual lives in a home and attends a school in which computers are a part of daily experience." (Botvin and Murray, 1975 p. 18).

The development of a valid and reliable method to characterize children's aptitude for computer-based technologies is also important for issues in both basic and applied research. The identification of particularly talented as well as disadvantaged youngsters in this area will be important in order to provide advanced or remedial training. The need to understand computer-based technologies will certainly increase in importance for almost all career choices. Thus, there is an immediate applied value to this kind of research development.

The study of children's computer aptitude is also important for more theoretical issues and basic research questions. In addition to advances in the characterization of knowledge organization across development, advances in the study of the inter-relation of social and cognitive processes may emerge from the study of children's peer interactions on the computer in problem-solving situations. The advances in cognitive growth and development due to peer conflict and interaction have been well documented (Ames and Murray, 1982; Botvin and Murray, 1975; Perret-Clermont, 1980; Smith, Johnson and Johnson, 1981) and are supported by several prominent theories of developmental psychology. These include the theories of Piaget (1965, 1977); Harry Stack Sullivan (1953) and Vygotsky (1962, 1977; Wertsch, 1985). See Damon (1985) for an extensive review of this area and a compelling argument concerning the potential of peer interactions for social and cognitive development.

The common finding from studies based on these rather diverse theories of social and cognitive development is that the communication of ideas in peer interaction is often more effective than adult-child interaction; ideas exchanged by peers appear to be evaluated more strategically and at a "deeper" level of representation. Questions as to the underlying mechanisms involved in the effectiveness of peer vs. adult-child interaction may be answered by a systematic examination of the computer-aptitude of peers and their interaction in computer tasks. These questions prompted a recent study by Burns and Ferguson (1986) in which a microgenetic analysis of peer interactions on a computer task was undertaken. Burns and Ferguson (1986) matched students for computer aptitude and knowledge using the CCAKT from the present study, and examined the types of exchanges during the completion of a popular piece of children's software called "Gertrude's Secrets". In subsequent studies, we hope to employ the CCAKT and match pairs of children in several types of aptitude relations (hi-lo, hi-hi, lo-lo) and record peer exchanges in order to further examine the inter-relation of social and cognitive processes across development.

In sum, the development of a measure of children's aptitude for computer-based technologies has both theoretical importance and applied value. The recognition of the importance of peer interaction in the educational curricula may, in fact, lead the school systems of the future to be sensitive to computer-aptitude and adopt extensive computer-based instruction and coursework that relies on extensive peer exchanges.

References

Alexander, P.A., Willson, V.L., White, C.S., & Fuqua, J.D. (1985). *Geometric analogy reasoning in young children*. Paper presented at the annual meeting of the American Educational Research Association, Chicago, Il.

Ames, G., & Murray, F.B. (1982). When two wrongs make a right: promoting cognitive change through social conflict. *Developmental Psychology*, **18**, 894–897.

Botvin, G., & Murray, F.B. (1975). The efficacy of peer modeling and social conflict in the acquisition of conservation. *Child Development*, **46**, 796–799.

Brillhart, L. (1980. Computers: An answer to engineering student learning styles at the community college. *Computers and Education*, **4**, 247–253.

Burns, B., and Ferguson, E. (1986). *Children's social interactions during problem-solving tasks on the computer: The effects of age, amount of computer experience, and problem difficulty.* Manuscript submitted to the Society for Research in Child Development Meetings, April 1987.

Damon, W. (1984). Peer education: The untapped potential. *Journal of Applied Developmental Psychology*, **5**, 331–343.

Johnson, R.T. (1972). Computer programmer aptitude battery. In O.K. Buros (Ed.) *The 7th Mental Measurements Yearbook*. Highland Park, N.J.: Gryphon Press.

Mandler, J. (1984). Representation. In P. Mussen (Ed.) *Handbook of Child Psychology*. New York: Wiley.

McKeithen, K.B., Reitman, J.S., Rueter, H.H., and Hirtle, S.C. (1981). Knowledge organization and skill differences in computer programmers. *Cognitive Psychology*, **13**, 307–325.

Miura, I. and Hess, R.D. (1983, August). *Sex differences in computer access, interest and usage.* Paper presented at the American Psychological Association Meeting, Anaheim, CA.

Perret-Clermont, A. (1980). *Social interaction and cognitive development in children.* London: Academic Press.

Piaget, J. (1965). *The moral judgement of the child.* New York: Free Press.

Piaget, J. (1977). *The development of thought.* New York: The Viking Press.

Poplin, M.S., Drew, D.E., and Gable, R.S. (1984). *Computer Aptitude Literacy and Interest Profile.* Austin, TX: PRO-ED.

Schmidt, F.L., Gast-Rosenberg, I. and Hunter, J.E. (1980). Validity generalization results for computer programmers. *Journal of Applied Psychology*, **65**, 643–661.

Smith, K., Johnson, D.W., and Johnson. R.T. (1981). Can conflict be constructive? Controversy versus concurrence seeking in learning groups. *Journal of Educational Psychology*, **73**, 651–663.

Sullivan, H.S. (1953). *The interpersonal theory of psychiatry.* New York: Norton.

Vygotsky, L.S. (1962). *Thought and language.* Cambridge, MA: M.I.T. Press.

Vygotsky, L.S. (1978). *Mind and society.* Cambridge, MA: Harvard University Press.

Wertsch, J.V., Ed.(1985). *Culture, communication, and cognition: Vygotskian perspectives.* New York: Cambridge University Press.

CHAPTER 4

Assessing Microcomputer Competencies for the Elementary Teacher: An Indepth Study of Illinois Schools

ROBERT C. MORRIS

and

EUGENE MEYER
Northern Illinois University

Concerned with current elementary school students' microcomputer competencies and skills, this study analyzes responses from administrators and teachers from elementary school districts in Illinois. Conducted in 1986, all 431 elementary school districts in the state of Illinois were surveyed. The questionnaire used identified: respondent biographical information and microcomputer training; school demographic data; perceived student ability, application and understanding levels; and desired future student levels of competencies.

This study reveals current elementary administrative/teacher perceptions about student microcomputer competence in the elementary school. Implications of this study range from a call for indepth microcomputer assessment activities within individual schools to developing means for acquiring better student understanding about microcomputer problems and increasing student involvement or interaction with microcomputer concerns. This study calls on all educators to begin determining exactly what "microcomputer knowledge" their students need in order to function effectively in the future.

KEY WORDS: Microcomputer literacy, elementary education, microcomputer competence, microcomputer curriculum/policy.

PROGRESS in many areas such as communications and medicine has brought unquestionable benefits in this century, but progress has also created an appalling capacity for self-destruction and an increased rate of social change. American education is "hooked" on progress, too. It dreams of panaceas—universal modern cures for the ancient pain of learning—easy ways to raise test scores, for example, and simultaneously prepare the "whole child" for his role in an ever-changing society. Education has become a tormented battleground where armies of theories clash, frequently phrased in language unintelligible to the layman. The multitude of theories often are based on social factors that stimulate growth and help dogma to sweep through the profession, changing standards, techniques, and procedures. These changes often dislocate students and teachers to little common purpose, and eventually they falter and are discarded.

The time has arrived when progress also dictates that micro-computer education must become an integral part of school curriculum. This highly controversial and crucial concern affects us all. As professionals, we must begin to cope realistically with the challenges and obstacles posed by the area of microcomputer education. As educators we need to realize that we must provide microcomputer education for all ages and socio-economic groups. Appropriate means of reaching our diverse population can and will be found as we become more convinced of its importance. Thornburg notes that "if we're to judge from recent advertisements, our children will be incapable of surviving in society unless they use computers in their classrooms and homes." Among the more reprehensible examples of this concern is a Commodore Computer commercial showing a young man rejected by a college, presumably because he hadn't had access to a Commodore 64 computer at home. Thorn-burg, of course, views the premise behind this type of advertising as false. "Although proper access to computer technology can be of tremendous value to students of all ages, the interaction of student and teacher is what facilitates most learning. In this light the computer is neutral—it is another educational tool, like a book. Whether this tool is used effectively or not is a human decision, one that not many people seem to know how to make." (Thornburg, 1985).

Given that the current technological base for our civilization is inherently transitory, depending on consumers, the environment, and non-renewable resources, what should a program stressing the basics of computer/microcomputer education entail? Part of the answer lies in improved microcomputer education for all ages and all socio-economic groups. Additionally, what kinds of instructional models must be identified to positively affect teachers' and students' development toward proper choices and use of computer resources?

STATEMENT OF THE PROBLEM

The purpose of this study was to become acquainted with the perceptions and ideas on current microcomputer problems held by elementary teachers and supervisors in the state of Illinois. Information related to those perceptions was gathered through a questionnaire and microcomputer competencies survey.

It is hoped that with a more thorough understanding of elementary faculty and supervisory perceptions concerning microcomputer problems, policy as well as curriculum planning can be more closely determined to meet the needs of the students. Instructional decisions for classroom use as well as school-wide microcomputer programs can be better coordinated as well as implemented if teacher competencies are determined.

Several anticipated contributions of this study should yield social benefit. First the investigation has produced information which can have direct impact on microcomputer education programs. The data, for example, includes in-depth analysis of attitudes concerning the use, development, and dissemenation of microcomputer knowledge that affect our public schools. Second, perceptions that have been identified can be used as ammunition for current policy and actions of authority groups. Finally, with better understanding of the attitudes of teachers and supervisors toward microcomputers, a more comprehensive model for dealing with various views of microcomputer education and microcomputer development and use can be put into motion in our elementary schools.

RELATED RESEARCH

A literature review reveals several factors related to educator perceptions of microcomputer competencies which appear to have the potential to influence various educational practices and curricular offerings in the school setting. This current study has identified four influential factors that are of value in assessing the levels of educator's understandings and competencies of the microcomputer and the problems surrounding it: 1) Microcomputer literacy is not well defined, despite the growth of the curricular focus, 2) Microcomputer literacy is low with little emphasis in teacher training programs, 3) Communication among microcomputer educators is poor, and 4) From the manufacturer's perspective, the educational computer market is a golden opportunity to make money.

Educators, especially for the past decade, have been and are continually operationalizing the definition of "computer literacy," as well as redefining the role of the microcomputer in the public school. These activities have resulted in a host of definitions for the term "computer literacy."

These various definitions of computer literacy tend to fall into three distinct categories. The first places an emphasis on the hardware/ programming concerns. The second definitional area stresses the awareness issues. Bitter and Camuse, in writing about the awareness aspects, state that computer awareness or, learning about computers, is "the ability to recognize computers, their capabilities, and limitations and includes developing an openness in dealing with computers" (Bitter & Camuse, 1984, p. 208). A third trend in definitions is to take a middle of the road perspective in which computer literacy is seen as a combination of both the awareness issues and programming abilities.

Gleason remarked that: "while there may be general agreement that computer literacy is the ability of an individual to understand and deal with computers, there is no consensus on the precise knowledge, skills, or attitudes that an individual needs to function adequately in a technological society" (Gleason, 1981, p. 4). This apparent lack of consensus prompted Beverly Hunter to analyze the definitions of computer literacy, and to compare them with a Rorschach test. She states that: "computer literacy is a phrase into which we project our values, our experiences, our skills, our visions of the future as it relates to technology, to computers, to communications, to information" (Hunter, 1983a, p. 8). A number of individuals have projected their values and visions of the future through their definitions of computer literacy during the late 1970's and early 1980's. Individuals such as Luehrmann, Hunter, Watt, Moursund, Charp, Levin, and those people associated with the Minnesota Educational Computing Consortium helped form many of the original ideas in developing the field of computer technology. Many definitions attempt to be comprehensive in nature; others are more narrow in scope. As well, some of the definitions mention the skills, attitudes or knowledges that a person who is computer literate should possess.

Those definitions that emphasize the hardware and programming concerns were most prevalent in the early 1970's.

Arthur Luehrmann first coined the term "computer literacy" during that period. Luehrmann's earliest definition of "computer literacy" was "the ability to do computing, and not merely to

recognize, identify, or be aware of alleged facts about computing"
(Luehrmann, 1981, p. 683). According to Luehrmann, "the long-
term goal of computer literacy is . . . the application of computer
knowledge and skills to traditional subjects taught in school"
(Luehrmann, 1984, p. 38). His idea of equating "doing computing"
with "computer literacy" has not been considered by some to be
comprehensive enough in nature. It does not adequately say what
computer literacy represents.

Another early advocate of the construct of computer literacy is
David Moursund. As editor of *The Computing Teacher*, he believes that
"computer literacy refers to a broad, integrated knowledge of low-
level computer science" (Moursund, 1976, p. 54). Moursund defines
microcomputer literacy as:

> A knowledge of the capabilities, limitations, applications, and possible effects of
> computers. Two levels of computer literacy are often discussed. The lower level is an
> awareness knowledge. The higher level is a functional or working knowledge
> (Moursund, 1980, p. 44).

Another individual who has done much to help shape the use of the
computer in education is Beverly Hunter. A senior staff scientist at the
Human Resources Research Organization, she has done much work
with developing and integrating computer literacy into the K-8
curriculum. She has written that computer literacy is discipline
dependent; that is, "the specific skills and knowledge students will
need will depend on what they'll be doing" (Levin, 1983a, p. 25). For
elementary and middle school level teachers, Hunter defines computer literacy as "the ability to use suitably programmed computers
in appropriate ways to assist in accomplishing tasks and solving
problems, and ability to make informed judgments about social and
ethical issues involving computers and communications systems"
(Hunter, 1981, p. 61). Computer literacy is seen as not just the
mastery of a body of knowledge, but also the ability to use the
computer efficiently in accomplishing a task. This idea is basically the
same one advanced in Computer literacy: problem-solving with
computers (Horn & Poirot, 1981, p. 20). These comprehensive
definitions tell what skills or knowledges the "computer literate"
should possess. Daniel Watt sees computer literacy as "that collection
of skills, knowledge, understanding, values and relationships that
allows a person to function comfortably as a productive citizen of a
computer-oriented society" (Masat, 1981, p. 26). His stance can be

considered one of the middle-of-the-road views. The same comprehensive idea has been expressed by others (Gawronski & West, 1982; Napier, 1983; Neill, 1976).

The National Council of Teachers of Mathematics (1980, 1983), believe that to be computer literate one must: 1) know the role of the computer in today's society, 2) how to use and communicate with them, and 3) how to command their services in problem solving. The Association for Educational Data Systems (AEDS) (1982) and the Committee on Computer Education of the Conference Board of the Mathematical Sciences (Carpenter, Corbett & Kepner 1980) have taken virtually the same stance. The pronouncements of these three associations have done much to influence individuals in the field, and create unity in definition.

Numerous studies (Masat, 1981; Gawronski & West, 1982, Thompson, 1982; Gaashell, 1982; Klassen, 1983; Scher, 1983, Trainor, 1984) have attempted to consolidate attitudes toward computer literacy and related issues. Only a few of the studies reported in the literature however, have been specifically related to the evaluation of educator knowledge regarding microcomputer literacy matters. None of the studies reported have been related specifically to microcomputer perceptions of elementary faculty and supervisors. The available studies of microcomputer issues, however, have provided a useful background for this study (Johnson, 1985; Slamkowski, 1986).

Johnson (1985) measured high school teacher's attitudes in relationship to selected "experts" in the region, while Slamkowski's study (1986) focused on nursing educators at the undergraduate level. Anderson, Klassen and Johnson's (1981) earlier study surveyed the attitudes of secondary teachers in the hard science areas, revealing that information collected from different academic teaching areas and from different grade levels differed significantly. This study also reported that 84% of those teachers responding believed that all secondary students should have a minimal understanding of computers. What constituted minimal was not defined.

The Minnesota Educational Computing Consortium (MECC, 1981) was involved in a study of microcomputer knowledge and attitudes of educators. The population included secondary school teachers. The findings suggested a general familiarity with terminology, with the idea that computers are an essential element in an educational system, and that problems exist in identifying common objectives. The MECC study findings also revealed that a limited number of those responding were adequately dealing with the supply and demand of microcomputer technology in our schools. This study also identifies how the subjects of the MECC'S study were not generally applying microcomputer technology and methods to their everyday life activities.

AIMS AND PROCEDURES

This investigation was designed to produce information that could have direct impact on microcomputer education programs in the elementary schools. It is hoped that once teacher's and administration's perceived ideas concerning the microcomputer have been established and addressed, that appropriate cognitive, effective, and psychomoter activities can be prescribed. A survey tool, developed to address the various comprehensive levels of the microcomputer and its technology, was designed using a Likert scale format (Likert, 1961, 1967).

A number of the items from the Johnson investigation's questionnaire (1984) as well as insights from the cognitive domain of thought developed by Benjamin Bloom *et al.* (1956) were studied to help formulate and construct this current study's questionnaire. No microcomputer research studies except Johnson's (1984) and Slamkowski (1986) have used items similar to this investigation's questionnaire.

Part I of the instrument includes questions related to School District Demographic Data. District size, numbers of microcomputer and software available, as well as certification and training are all identified. Part II of the questionnaire includes questions related to individual socio-biographical background, interests, and observations. Part II contains five separate sections: A "General" response area; "Education and the Microcomputer"; "Programming"; "Society and the Microcomputer" and "Demonstration of Competencies." The General area has 4 items while the other 3 areas contain from 5 to 10 items. These five sections together afford a range of two possible responses for each question. These include responses that indicate at what "Present" grade level that certain activity is being implemented and a second response that indicates a possible "Future" grade level of implementation for the identified activity.

The present study includes results of a questionnaire distributed to all 431 Elementary School Districts in the State of Illinois. A total of 265 elementary school districts responded to the questionnaire representing 593 elementary schools.

Data collected were analyzed through absolute frequencies. Of the 265 questionnaires returned, 100 percent of the total returned contained sufficient responses for inclusion in the study. All returned responses are included in Tables 1 and 2, while some respondents did not complete certain items in Tables 3 and 4. Table 1 includes respondent information and microcomputer training. Table 2 includes School Demographic Data. Both Tables 1 and 2 are divided into Public or Private categories. Tables 3 and 4 display perceived student ability, application, and understanding levels as presently perceived by the respondents and as desired for future levels of competence, also as perceived by the respondents.

Table 1   Respondent's Micro-Information & Micro-Training

		Public	*Private*
I.	Respondent's Work Situation Position: (N = 265)		
	A. Classroom Teacher	22 (8.3%)	1
	B. Library/Media Specialist	13 (4.9%)	0
	C. Coordinator/Supervisor/Director	40 (15.1%)	0
	D. Principal	92 (34.7%)	1
	E. Superintendent	68 (25.6%)	0
	F. Assistant Superintendent	24 (9.1%)	0
	G. Administrative Assistant	3 (1.1%)	0
	H. Computer Lab Teacher	1 (.4%)	0
		Public	*Private*
II.	Respondent's Microcomputer Training (more than one category could be identified)		
	A. Coursework	126	2
	B. Self-taught	158	1
	C. In-service	177	1
	D. Workshop	11	0
	E. Other	13	0
	F. None	10	0

RESULTS: COMPETENCY LEVELS AND PERCEPTIONS ABOUT MICROCOMPUTERS IN THE ELEMENTARY SCHOOL CURRICULUM

The findings of this research study reveal the following:

I.   *Respondent's Work Situations*: Two Hundred Sixty-Five elementary school districts in Illinois of the 431 responded to the questionnaire (61·5%). Of those responding, a majority of those actually answering the questionnaire (69·4%) were either the elementary district superintendent, an assistant superintendent or an elementary principal. Twenty-two (8·3%) classroom teachers, 13 (4·9%) Library/Media Specialist and 40 (15·1%) curriculum coordinators responded. Of the 265 respondents only two were private schools.

II. *Respondent's Microcomputer Training:* Here an attempt was made to identify the various types of microcomputer training respondents might have. Respondents could check more than one category. Four Hundred and Ninety-Nine categories were checked by the 265 respondents.

Table 2

School Demographic Data

		Public	Private	Total
I.	Number of Elementary Schools Represented	593	2	595
II.	Size of Schools (N = 595)			
	a. Under 1000 students	246 (41.3%)	2 (.7%)	248
	b. Over 1000 students	347 (58.3%)	0	347
III.	Total Number of Microcomputers in Elementary Schools represented (Number of Schools)	4464 (204)	12 (2)	4476 (206)
IV.	Total Number of Microcassettes or Microdisks in Elementary Schools represented (Number of Schools)	37,773 (192)	70 (2)	37,843 (194)

The data displayed in Table 2 are demographics about the elementary schools represented by the respondents:

I.   *Number of Elementary Schools Represented:* Some districts contain more than one elementary school. 61·5% of the elementary school districts in Illinois responded, representing approximately 21·9% (593) of the elementary public schools operating in 1986.

II. *Size of Schools*: A slight majority (58·3%) of the schools are well over 1000 students while 246 have populations under 1000.

III. *Total Number of Microcomputers in Elementary Schools*: Two Hundred and Four schools reported 4,464 microcomputers in their schools (that's approximately 22 micros per school).

IV. *Total Number of Microcassettes or Microdisks in the Elementary Schools Surveyed:* Of the 595 elementary schools represented, 192 have either Microcassettes or Microdisks.

The data in Tables 3 and 4 are responses to 14 opinion questions. Table 3 asked each respondent about their "Present Student Microcomputer Competencies," while Table 4 asks the same questions but in the context of "Prospected Future Student Microcomputer Competencies." Each table has four separate grade levels for identifying competency levels. Tables 3 and 4 were also grouped into three sections: "Programming Abilities"; "Application" and "Understanding," with five questions in the first two sections and four questions in the "Understanding" section.

Under the section topic "Present Programming Abilities," the five individual questions asked were: 1) "Knows variety of uses for microcomputer"; 2) "Can use microcomputer to assist in learning"; 3) "Knows various types of computer assisted instruction"; 4) "Uses computers without software"; and 5) "Applies microcomputer for individual and creative needs." Under Section I average respondent opinions about "Present" student "Programming Abilities" reveal that 35·6% of the respondents feel that students in grades K-4 presently have various programming ability levels. While 64·4% of those responding feel that students at the 5th and 6th grade levels currently have various "programming ability" levels.

Section II, titled "Application," asks respondents five questions concerning present student applications. They are: 1) "Writes in simple logo"; 2) "Writes in simple BASIC"; 3) "Programs in

Table 3   Present Student Microcomputer Competencies

Grade Levels

I. Programming Abilities	K-3	4	5	6
1. Knows variety of uses for microcomputer (N = 116)	37(22.4%)	45(27.3%)	37(22.4%)	46(27.9%)
2. Can use microcomputer to assist in learning (N = 132)	38(27.1%)	35(25.0%)	29(20.8%)	38(27.1%)
3. Knows various types of computer assisted instruction (N = 117)	49(32.0%)	37(24.2%)	30(19.6%)	37(24.2%)
4. Uses computers without software (N = 119)	13(10.7%)	23(19.0%)	36(29.8%)	49(40.5%)
5. Applies microcomputer for individual and creative needs (N = 136)	16(13.6%)	26(22.0%)	31(26.3%)	45(38.1%)

II Application				
1. Writes in simple Logo (N = 127)	20(22.5%)	24(27.0%)	18(20.2%)	27(30.3%)
2. Writes in simple BASIC (N = 118)	3(02.5%)	29(24.0%)	34(28.1%)	55(45.4%)
3. Programs in PASCAL, COBOL, or FORTRAN (N = 72)	0(0.00%)	0(0.00%)	0(0.00%)	6(100%)
4. Programs with Low-Res Graphics (N = 98)	1(01.5%)	12(17.9%)	16(23.9%)	38(56.7%)
5. Works with flow-charting (N = 105)	0(0.00%)	6(12.5%)	11(22.9%)	31(64.6%)

III. Understanding				
1. Discusses the future of computing (N = 115)	10(09.9%)	22(21.8%)	25(24.8%)	44(43.5%)
2. Discusses robatics and artificial intelligence (N = 110)	2(04.2%)	5(10.4%)	10(20.8%)	31(64.6%)
3. Is aware of social impact of microcomputer (N = 109)	7(08.5%)	22(26.8%)	22(26.8%)	31(37.8%)
4. Is aware of careers available because of the computer (N = 117)	14(12.7%)	25(22.8%)	24(21.8%)	47(42.7%)

C

Table 4   Prospected Future Student Microcomputer Competencies

Grade Levels

I. Programming Abilities	K-3	4	5	6
1. Knows variety of uses for microcomputer (N = 116)	52(44.8%)	26(22.4%)	15(12.9%)	23(19.9)
2. Can use microcomputer to assist in learning (N = 132)	50(37.9%)	35(26.5%)	16(12.1%)	31(23.5%)
3. Knows various types of computer assisted instruction (N = 117)	50(42.7%)	28(23.9%)	17(14.5%)	22(18.9%)
4. Uses computers without software (N = 119)	43(36.1%)	32(26.9%)	23(19.3%)	21(17.7%)
5. Applies microcomputer for individual and creative needs (N = 136)	55(40.4%)	23(16.9%)	18(13.2%)	40(29.5%)

II. Application				
1. Writes in simple Logo (N = 127)	61(48.0%)	22(17.3%)	15(11.8%)	29(22.9%)
2. Writes in simple BASIC (N = 118)	45(38.1%)	21(17.9%)	24(20.3%)	28(23.7%)
3. Programs in PASCAL, COBOL, or FORTRAN (N = 72)	26(36.1%)	3(04.2%)	6(08.3%)	37(51.4%)
4. Programs with Low-Res Graphics (N = 98)	32(32.7%)	11(11.2%)	15(15.3%)	40(40.8%)
5. Works with flow-charting (N = 105)	32(30.5)	12(11.4)	17(16.2)	44(41.9)

III. Understanding				
1. Discusses the future of computing (N = 115)	36(31.3%)	18(15.7%)	15(13.0%)	46(40.0%)
2. Discusses robotics and artificial intelligence (N = 110)	34(30.9%)	6(05.5%)	21(19.1%)	49(44.5%)
3. Is aware of social impact of microcomputer (N = 109)	32(29.4%)	17(15.6%)	21(19.3%)	39(35.8%)
4. Is aware of careers available because of the computer (N = 117)	31(26.5%)	20(17.1%)	17(14.5%)	49(41.9%)

PASCAL, COBOL, or FORTRAN"; 4) "Programs with Low-Res Graphics"; and 5) "Works with flow-charting." Average respondent opinions under Section II about "Present" student "Application" reveals that respondents feel that approximately 28·8% of students in grades K-4 have various application abilities. While 71·2% of those responding feel that students at the 5th and 6th grade levels currently have various "application" abilities.

Section III, titled "Understanding," asks respondents four questions concerning present student understandings about the microcomputer. Those questions are: 1) "Discusses the future of computing" 2) "Discusses robotics and artificial intelligence"; 3) "Is aware of social impact of microcomputer"; 4) "Is aware of careers available because of the computer." Average respondent opinions under Section III about "Present" student "Understanding" reveals that respondents feel that approximately 31·4% of students in grades K-4 have various understanding levels. While 68·6% of those responding feel that students at the 5th and 6th grade levels currently have various "Understanding" levels.

Table 4, "Prospected Future Student Microcomputer Competencies," utilizes the same three sections and questions for predictive purposes. This table asks respondents to project at what grade level they "would like" to see the microcomputer ability or skill under question implemented. Under Section I, "Programming Abilities," an average respondent opinion of 63·5% predict that K-4th grade students in their district will eventually have various programming abilities. While 36·5% of those responding predict that 5th and 6th grade students in their district will eventually have various "programming abilities."

Section II of Table 4, titled "Application," asks for predicted grade levels of application for elementary students. Average respondent opinions indicate that 63·5% of those responding predict that students in the K-4th grades in their districts will in the future have various "programming abilities." As well, 36·5% of those responding feel that students at the 5th and 6th grade levels in their districts will in the future have various "application" abilities.

Section III of Table 4, titled "Understanding," deals with elementary student understandings about the microcomputer and its impact on society as perceived by responding teachers and administrators. Average respondent opinions indicate that 43·1% of those responding predict that students in the K-4th grades in their districts will in the future have various knowledges and "Understandings" about the social impact of microcomputerization. As well, 56·9% of those responding predict that students at the 5th and 6th grade levels in their districts will in the future have various "understandings" concerning microcomputerization within our society.

DISCUSSION AND CONCLUSIONS

Table 3, "Present Student Microcomputer Competencies," addresses itself to various opinions about elementary students' microcomputer competencies. The questionnaire items attempted to differentiate between degrees of insight on the part of the respondents, and specifically to particular microcomputer issues posed. Additionally, the questions posed attempt to determine if there are relationships between administrator/teacher perceptions and their understandings about actual student microcomputer competencies.

The data indicate some interesting perspectives currently held by administrators. When asked what grade levels of elementary students "know a variety of uses for microcomputers?", over 49·7% (82) responded that their K thru 4th graders have some competencies for programming at various levels, while 50·3% (83) responded that only their 5th through 6th graders have various degrees of programming abilities. In the same vain 52·1% (72) of those responding believe that their K thru 4th graders already are using the "microcomputer to assist them in learning." While the remaining 47·9% (67) of those responding perceive only their 5th and 6th grade students as presently using the microcomputer as an aid for learning.

On the other hand only 29·7% (36) of those questioned believe that their K thru 4th graders can use a microcomputer without software and only 25·6% (42) of those surveyed believe that their K thru 4th graders presently apply the microcomputer for their individual and/or creative purposes. Another question asked under "Section I—Programming Abilities" identified 46·2% (86) of those responding believe that their K thru 4th graders presently work with various degrees of microcomputer assisted instruction.

The above are all interesting results given the large amount of publicity both teachers and students have received over the past few years concerning their lack of understanding of computer technology (Thornburg, 1985). It seems that the teachers and administrators who responded to the questionnaire hold somewhat optomistic views of what their elementary students programming abilities are. As well, when comparing "Section I—Present Programming Abilities" from Table 3 to "Section I—Prospected Future Programming Abilities" of Table 4 it becomes very evident that those responding feel that in the near future elementary students in the lower grades (K thru 4th) will be much more competent. Table 4 reveals that 67·2% of those responding feel that children in the K thru 4th grades will, in the near future, know various uses for the microcomputer. Additionally, 64·4% of those responding feel that K thru 4th graders will in the near future be using the microcomputer as an aid to learning. As well, 66·6% of those responding feel that K thru 4th graders will soon know numerous types of computer assisted instruction. Other "Programming Abilities" will also increase for the elementary students at the K thru 4th grade levels. Among them will be the abilities to apply the microcomputer for individual and creative needs. Here 57·3% of those responding predict an increase.

Likewise Table 3's "Section II—Present Student Applications" and "Section III—Present Student Understandings" reflect the *perceived* relatively low K thru 4th grade application levels and minimal student understandings about the microcomputer. While their counter parts in Table 4, "Section II—Prospected Future Student Applications" and "Section III—Prospected Future Student Understandings" predict both a *rapid and successful growth* for the lower grades (K thru 4th) in the application and general understandings concerning the microcomputer and microcomputer technologies. Individual questionnaire items in Sections II and III of Tables 3 and 4 attempt to differentiate between degrees of insight on the part of the respondent, or specifically to a certain microcomputer issue posed to the respondents. Additionally the questions attempted to determine if there is general concencus concerning administrative/faculty opinions and attitudes, and actual student microcomputer competencies.

In summary, a majority of the study respondents were aware that there are dramatic changes and effects of computerization within their schools and within individual grade levels. This degree of awareness is important, given that 5 out of every 6 responding identified increased future student programming abilities, application, and understandings. Only slightly fewer than 17% of those responding felt that their student's abilities, application and understandings will not be increased in the near future.

The overall levels of microcomputer literacy generally identified shows that students in the lower grades (K-4th) are less aware of the microcomputer than are those in the higher grades (5th and 6th). Teachers need then to be made aware of these facts. Instructional modes need to be developed for each grade level which can positively affect attitudes toward better competencies, understandings and use of the microcomputer. Consequently, more than ever, educators need to identify better the various microcomputer literacy levels within their student populations. To label students, for example, as "knowledgeable" about microcomputer problems and concerns without formal microcomputer educational experiences is detrimental to the whole concept of educating to the social realities of the day. By fighting the tendency to allow the "mass Media," various and often confusing "expert" opinion, as well as pressure group reasoning to be the sole sources of microcomputer education for our students, we can possibly create a well-informed and "microcomputer-minded" population.

Microcomputer education must be an outgoing activity, in which current and emerging knowledge is constantly shared and updated. Microcomputer education programs to be effective, must therefore relate to the myriad of attitudes and values students carry into decision-making. If teachers can provide opportunities for students to explore their values, the decision-making process can be relatively bias free.

The findings of this study are by no means comprehensive. A number of its implications can help to create more meaningful teacher involvement in working with microcomputer-related matters, however. An array of implications for educators are as follows: (1) conduct microcomputer-related assessment activities within schools, (2) develop means for acquiring better understandings on the part of students for microcomputer problems, and (3) increase student involvement or interaction on microcomputer concerns.

Additionally, educators should determine the microcomputer knowledge students need in order to function effectively in the future. Under these conditions, teachers may be better able to contribute their expertise to devising programs that can provide young people with the best possible opportunities for understanding microcomputer problems.

References

Anderson, R.E., Klassen, D.L., and Johnson, D.C. (1981, December). In defense of a comprehensive view of computer literacy—a reply to Luehrmann. *Mathematics Teacher*, 687–690.

Association for Educational Data Systems. (1982). *AEDS proceedings: The tomorrow in new technology: Frontiers in administrative computing; adventures in instructional computing.* Washington, D.C.: Association for Educational Data Systems. (ERIC Document Reproduction Service No. ED 223 239).

Bitter, G. and Camuse, R.A. (1984). *Using a microcomputer in the classroom.* Reston, VA: Reston Publishing Company.

Bloom, B. (1956). Taxonomy of Educational Objectives: Handbook I: Cognitive Domain. New York: Longman, Inc.

Carpenter, T.D., Corbett, M.K., and Kepner, H.S., Jr., Lindquist, M.M., and Reyes, R.E. (1980, September). The current status of computer literacy: NAEP results for secondary students. *Mathematics Teacher*, 669–673.

Gawronski, J.D., and West, C.E. (1982, October). Computer literacy. *ASCD Curriculum Update*, 1–3.

Gauschell, H. (1982). *Microcomputers in education.* (ERIC Document Reproduction Service No. ED 225 540).

Gleason, G.T. (1981, March). Microcomputers in education: The state of the art. *Educational Technology*, 4–18.

Horn, C.A. and Poirot, J.L. (1981). *Computer literacy: Problem-solving with computers.* Austin, TX: Sterling Swift.

Hunter, B. (1981, September). Computer literacy in grades K-8 *Journal of Educational Technology Systems*, 59–66.

Hunter, B. (1983). *My students use computers.* Reston, VA: Reston Publishing Company.

Johnson, S.R. (1984). An investigation of microcomputer literacy skills for public secondary school teachers in South Carolina. Diss. University of South Carolina.

Johnson, S.R. (1985). An investigation of microcomputer literacy skills for public secondary school teachers in South Carolina. University of South Carolina. Unpublished manuscript.

Klassen, D. (1983, May). Computer literacy: What it is and how to get it. *School Business Affairs*, 44–45.

Levin, D. (1983, March). Everybody wants "computerliteracy," so maybe we should know what it means. *American School Board Journal*, 25–28.

Likert, R. (1961). *The patterns of management.* New York: McGraw-Hill Book Company.

Likert, R. (1967). *The human organizations: its management and value.* New York: McGraw-Hill Book Company.

Luehrmann, A. (1984, April). Computer literacy. *Electronic Learning*, 38–40.

Luehrmann, A. (1981, December). Computer literacy—what should it be? *Mathematics Teacher*, 682–686.

Masat, F.E. (1981). *Computer literacy in higher education.* (AAHE/Higher Education Research Report No. 6, 1981). Washington, D.C.: American Association for Higher Education and Eric Clearinghouse on Higher Education. (ERIC Document Reproduction Service No. ED 214 446).

Minnesota Educational Computing Consortium. (1981). *Computer literacy study—an update.* St. Paul, MN: The author.

Moursund, D. (1980). *School Administrator's introduction to instructional use of computers.* Eugene, OR: International Council for Computers in Education.

Napier, J.D. (1983). Computer literacy and social studies teacher education. (Paper presented at the annual meeting of the Social Science Education Consortium). (ERIC Document Reproduction Service No. ED 231 740).

National Council of Teachers of Mathematics. (1983). *Teaching with microcomputers.* Reston, VA: National Council of Teachers of Mathematics.

Neill, M.J. (1976). *Recommendations for implementing computer literacy in Oregon secondary schools.* Salem, OR: Oregon State Department of Education. (ERIC Document Reproduction Service No. ED 217 866).

Scher, R.A. (1984). The computer backlash: How fear and misunderstanding are giving computer literacy a bad name. *Electronic Learning,* **12**(3), 22–24.

Slamkowski, D.J. (1986). Perceptions of nursing deans concerning current and future microcomputer literacy in their baccalaureate degree program. Diss. Northern Illinois University.

Thornburg, D. (1985). *The boiling cauldron. A Magazine,* 32–35.

Thompson, C.J. (1982). *Integrating computer literacy into the curriculum.* In Silvey, L. and Smart, J.R. (Eds.). *Mathematics for the middle grades (5–9).* Reston, VA: National Council of Teachers of Mathematics.

Trainor, T.N. (1984). *Computer literacy: Concepts and applications.* Santa Cruz, CA: Mitchell Publishing.

CHAPTER 5

Young Children's Interaction
With a Microcomputer

STEVEN B. SILVERN

PETER A. WILLIAMSON

and

TERRY M. COUNTERMINE
Auburn University

While research on the effects of computers in classrooms and the effects of teaching computer languages is burgeoning, the question of how children interact "naturally" with a computer has not been researched. In order to observe children's interaction with a computer, an Apple II was placed in a university laboratory school classroom. Thirty-nine children were allowed free access to the computer during center time and detailed observational logs were kept of the children's interaction with the computer. It was determined from this base study that computer play for young children is an initial step in computer literacy.

KEY WORDS: Computer language, computer literacy, computer play, microcomputer.

AMONG forward looking educators, the microcomputer is seen as the coming educational tool (Shalaway, 1980). But, as in all fields using computers, technology is far ahead of application. Educators are currently "casting about" in search of how computers may best be used in classrooms (Malone & Levin, 1981). Several research studies have looked at the effects of computers in the classroom (e.g., Instructional Use of Microcomputers Project, 1980), the effects of teaching children programming language (e.g., Siedman, 1981), and the effects of an informal learning environment, "microworld" (Loop, 1982). These studies use existing hardware and courseware to evaluate the effects of microcomputers assuming that use of the computer by children approximates mature computer/human interaction. Yet, little is known about *how* children interact with the computer. It is conceivable that the findings regarding the effectiveness of the microcomputer are being affected by the attitude/

approach children take with the computer. According to Ritchey and Armstrong (1981) there is no data on how children go about using microcomputers.

The study of how children interact with the computer can take two foci: one, software design features which attract children to computer games (Malone, 1980, 1981); and two, actual selection and manipulation of software and hardware (Levin & Cole, 1981). Malone (1980) surveyed children to determine which computer games they preferred. He then analyzed the most popular games to determine what made the games fun. Malone's analysis led to the hypothesis that factors involving challenge, fantasy, and curiosity combined to make games fun. This hypothesis was then tested with variations of Breakout (Malone, 1980) and Darts (Malone, 1981). Malone concluded that software designers should design materials which incorporate challenge, fantasy, and curiosity.

By surveying children, Malone analyzed games strictly on a self report basis. No attempt was made to observe children in the process of playing games. Also, games were analyzed completely on the intrinsic features of the game, for example, goal, score totaled, audio effects, randomness, response item. None of the games were analyzed based on extrinsic features. Malone's conclusions were based on complex variations of two extremely popular games and completely ignored the possibility of other factors or games to which children may react differently. Further, the experimental environment required children to play one of only two games, thus limiting the possibility of observing any other factors which may be at work in children's selection of games.

Levin and Cole (1981) briefly described observations of children interacting with computers in classroom settings and in computer clubs. They concluded that social resources, particularly peers, are critical factors in designing educational uses of the computer.

Studies examining how children use computers ought to preceed studies of effects of computers on children. Yet, we have little information on children's use of computers. The purpose of the present study was to observe children's "natural" use of a micro processor. Given the *choice* of using a computer in a stimulus rich environment, how would young children approach and manipulate a computer? The answer to this question should provide some insight for software developers as well as for researchers who wish to determine the impact/effects of specific computer interventions.

METHOD

Subjects

Thirty-nine children were enrolled in the Auburn University Early Education Summer Laboratory School program. The ages of the children ranged between 3 years 10 months and 7 years 11 months. The majority of the children were 5 and 6 years of age. Twenty-seven children were Caucasian and 2 were Oriental. Most of the children's parents were faculty members or university students. All of the children had previous group educational experiences, and all had access to educationally enriched environments. Table 1 reports the number of students by age and sex.

Table 1   Frequency of Children in Lab School Reported by Sex and Age

	Sex		
Age	Boys	Girls	Total
4 years	5	5	10
5 years	7	5	12
6 years	3	7	10
7 years	5	2	7
Total	20	19	39

Equipment

One Apple II microcomputer, consisting of the central processing unit, one disk drive, a color video monitor, and two game paddles, was placed on a table with two chairs facing the microcomputer keyboard and monitor. Two diskettes were available for use with the Apple (both diskettes were in paper folders resting on top of the disk drive to the left of the central processing unit). One diskette contained Penny Arcade (Budge, 1979), Animal Learning Game (Wigginton, 1978), Pinball (Kellner, 1977), Othello (n.a., 1978), Safecracker (Silas, 1978), Battleship (n.a., n.d.), Towers of Hanoi (Lambert,

1978), Noah's Ark (n.a., n.d.) Sink the Ship (n.a., 1978), Slot Machine (Carter, 1978), Blackjack (Legg, 1978), and Depth Charge (Waller, 1978). The second diskette contained Super Invader Cosmos (Astor International, n.d.). The games were chosen to provide a mix of games requiring two players versus games requiring one player, games which required the use of paddles versus games which required the use of the keyboard, games which required manipulative skill and timing strategies versus games which required intellectual strategies, and games which required reading ability versus games which required no reading ability.

Environment

The summer school laboratory during the regular school year is two partitioned college classrooms containing adult sized tables (not desks) and chairs, large vertical metal bookshelves, and 8 foot high metal and wood cabinets. During the summer quarter these two rooms are converted into a large open space with very little furniture, with most activities taking place on rugs and carpet squares. Between 10 and 15 centers take the place of the shelves and cabinets. Centers include dramatic play/dress-up, puppets, listening, reading, music, sand/water/blocks, construction, discovery, manipulative games, art, and cooking. Special centers incorporating specific content are also included. Also identified as a center was the computer center.

At least 1 hour a day was identified as center time. Children could choose any center on a space available basis. Since the computer center had two chairs, only two children could be in the computer center at any given time. Under these restrictions, center time was free choice; children were not assigned to centers. Children attended the summer lab 4 days per week for four weeks, thus allowing for 16 hours of observation.

Observation

Two senior pre-service education students kept a detailed observation log (Appendix A) of the children's interaction with the computer and interaction with each other. Observations were made only during scheduled center time even though the Apple was in use during other times of the day. All events occurring at the center during center time were recorded. Inter-observer reliability was determined by agreements divided by total observations; reliability was .63.

RESULTS AND DISCUSSION

Users

One-third of the children enrolled in the lab used the computer. Eighty-five percent of the users were boys, with five

Table 2   Computer Users Reported by Sex and Age

Age	Sex		Total
	Boys	Girls	
4 years	1	1	2
5 years	4	0	4
6 years	1	1	2
7 years	5	0	5
Total	11	2	13

and seven year olds providing the majority of use. A comparison of Tables 1 and 2 indicates that all the 7-year-old boys used the computer while only 57% of the 5-year-old boys and considerably fewer children in other groups used the computer.

   These results may be a function of the fact that only one microcomputer was available for use. The pattern for controlling the computer consisted of an interesting ritual frequently observed in schools when children are excited about a particular activity. Center time always followed group meeting time. As the teacher in charge of meeting began to give signs that the meeting was over, children began to inch their way toward the computer center. Since the children were seated on the floor, the move toward the center consisted of a series of short, quick slides along the floor. It appeared that the children tried to be subtle about this movement because it generally occurred when the teacher's eye gaze was directed away from the "movers/scooters" and stopped when eye gaze was directed toward them. Once in close proximity to the chairs in front of the screen, physical space was reserved by resting an elbow or draping an arm across the seat of the chair. As the teacher indicated the end of circle time, the chairs were occupied by a jump off the floor directly into the chair, reminiscent of two children going for the last chair in musical chairs. If two bottoms hit the seat at the same time, then the most powerful of the two took control of the chair. The final jump to the chair usually took place in teacher's mid-sentence. For example, Teacher: "All right, we're going to have center time from now" (children jump into chairs) "until 10:30." Since research has indicated that young girls are not as aggressive as young boys, this ritual may have been instrumental in keeping the girls away from the computer.

While 7-year-old users were chronic users (there was never any doubt as to where to find these children), the remainder of the children seemed to rotate between the computer and other available centers.

Using the Computer

No formal, whole group instruction was used to teach the children how to use the computer. Instructions on how to boot the computer were posted on the wall. Most of the games had instructions on how to play as part of the introductory frames. The observers were instructed to allow the children to use trial and error strategies when working with the computer. Unfortunately, the observers could not bear to reject a child's plea for help and generally told the children exactly what to do in order to boot the computer and to play the games. This was true even with our most precocious children and most skillful readers.

Initially (during the first week), children booted the Apple at the end of every game; even if they were going to play the same game again. They tended to ignore instructions within the game (e.g., "DO YOU WANT TO PLAY AGAIN?"). In regard to the parenthetical prompt, some children responded verbally; then booted the Apple. By the second week, the children had learned to boot the machine only at the beginning. In fact, they began to incorporate a "pre-booting" strategy. Sometime during the morning, one of the children—generally a 7-year-old, but sometimes a 5-year-old—would boot the machine, command the Apple to run a particular game, and then turn the monitor off; leaving the central unit on. When it was center time, the children simply turned the monitor on and begin playing the game that was already in progress. (The noise level of the room was generally high enough to mask the beeps made by the games while the monitor was off.)

During the first week social pressure was used to have paddle controlled games. No distinction seemed to be made between one player and two player games. Two children were always observed manipulating both paddles even though only one child was, in reality, playing. During the second week this changed. Children waiting to play demanded that two player games be played. Whenever one player games were in use, onlooker comments of "that's not fair" and "hurry up" were recorded.

Also during the second week, the children established a rotation system for the computer. The player in front of the keyboard was identified as champ and the other player was the challenger. Champ chose the game, and if applicable, the difficulty level. Whenever a game was over, the loser was replaced by the next in line. Any challenger who won then became champ.

Prior to the study it was predicted that the children would play lower order games and progress to more complex games with experience. It was also predicted that the children would tire of the video game mode and search for other ways to use the computer. There were no observations to indicate that this was the case. Perhaps the social interaction/rotation precluded such use of the machine. Another block to the predicted progression might be the limited access children had to the machine. In any case, the machine was used only in the video game mode.

One interesting social user of the computer was the 4-year-old girl. She sat in the chair next to her "boyfriend" (child's term), turned the paddle, and chatted at him. Her attention was focused on the boy and not on the monitor screen nor on the game paddle. She showed no reaction when she failed to hit the ball and showed no indication that she realized she was not in control of the pinball game. It appeared that the reason she was in the center was because somebody else was in the center.

The center was originally located in the quiet area of the room (between the reading and listening centers). By the second week the center was moved so that it was in the noisy area of the room. It was obvious to anyone in our wing of the building that, based on the shouting (e.g., oh boy, yay, holly molly, darn), the Apple was in use.

Table 3 presents the frequency of specific game use. Frequency of use rather than frequency of time of use was preferred because a powerful individual monopolizing pinball would mask the actual involvement of other children with the machine.

Table 3　Frequency of Game Use Reported by Sex and Age

Game	Boys 4	5	6	7	Girls 4	5	6	7	Total
Animal	—	—	—	—	—	—	—	—	0
Pinball	—	4	1	11	1	—	—	—	17
Othello	—	—	—	3	—	—	—	—	3
Safecracker	—	—	—	—	—	—	—	—	0
Battleship	1	2	—	7	—	—	—	—	10
Towers	—	—	—	—	—	—	—	—	0
Sink Ship	—	—	—	1	—	—	—	—	1
Slot Machine	—	—	—	—	—	—	—	—	0
Blackjack	—	—	—	—	—	—	—	—	0
Depthcharge	—	—	—	—	—	—	—	—	0
Invaders	2	2	—	2	—	—	—	—	6
Arcade	2	22	1	30	3	—	2	—	60
Hangman	—	5	—	—	—	—	—	—	5
Total	5	35	2	54	4	0	2	0	102

Table 3 clearly indicates the supremacy of the older boys and the overwhelming popularity of the "pong" type Penny Arcade games.

Table 3 also demonstrates that very little experimenting went on. Out of 13 games, 6 were never looked at and 10 games were played a total of 15 times. Which means that 3 games, Penny Arcade, Pinball, and Battleship, accounted for 85% of computer use.

While the paddle and ball games were popular, none of the children demonstrated mastery of the paddle. Games were won because of the failure of an opponent rather than the ability to use a clever strategy in making a return difficult. Many points were lost before either opponent applied the paddle to the ball.

Game Characteristics

The 13 available games were categorized on the following attributes: number of players required (1 or 2), hardware (keyboard or game paddles), strategy required (manipulative or cognitive), and reading required (reading necessary or unnecessary in order to play). This provided 16 possible cells, and with only 13 games available, several cells (9) were empty. No games were classified as two player keyboard games. Similarly, there were no manipulative strategy games which required reading. The bottom of Table 4 provides the features of the games used.

Table 4 reports the frequency of game use according to game characteristics. Penny Arcade, a two-player, paddle, manipulative, nonreading game, received the most play. Battleship and Hangman were the only games requiring reading that received any play. Other reading games such as Safecracker, Animal Learning, and Blackjack received no play. Eighty-five percent of all games played were nonreading and 82% of all games played were manipulative. The heavy use of Penny Arcade accounts for both of these figures. These observations suggest that several game characteristics might be manipulated in order to determine if these characteristics determine game use. For example, would Penny Arcade be used as much if manipulation of the paddle were effected through a touch sensitive screen or digits typed on the keyboard?

Table 4   Frequency of Game Play Reported by Game Characteristic

| | Two player | | One player | | |
	Paddle	Keyboard	Paddle	Keyboard	Total
Manipulative					
Nonreading	60	–	23	1	84
Reading	–	–	–	–	0
Cognitive					
Nonreading	3	–	–	–	3
Reading	–	–	–	15	15
Total	63	–	23	16	102

Penny Arcade = two player, paddle, manipulative, nonreading
Pinball, Slot Machine, Depthcharge, Invaders = 1 player, paddle, manipulative, nonreading
Sink the Ship = one player, keyboard, manipulative, nonreading
Othello = two player, paddle, cognitive, nonreading
Towers of Hanoi = one player, keyboard, cognitive, nonreading
Safecracker = two player, paddle, cognitive, reading
Animal Learning, Battleship, Blackjack, Hangman = one player, keyboard, cognitive, reading

CONCLUSION

While studies are already underway to determine the effects of computer use and the effects of specific programs on children's learning, little is known about how children use computers. Levin and Cole (1981) have noted that computers provide a special social interaction, and Malone (1981) has indicated that challenge, fantasy, and curiosity are important factors in program design. No other data has been reported on children's use of the microcomputer.

The present study observed children's use of the computer in a free choice environment. Some questions were: Who would use the computer, how would it be used, and what would be the characteristics of games used? Our observations indicated that primary users were older and more physically powerful boys. The computer was used in a video-game format. Once the popular games were identified and a system for playing was arranged, virtually all exploration of the machine stopped. Lastly, given free choice, the characteristics most popular were two person, paddle, manipulative, nonreading games. Obviously, these conclusions are intimately interrelated. Since the Apple was dominated by older boys, it is not astonishing that the games and features of the games would reflect interests that these boys might have. However, this is exactly what we had hoped to find in conducting this study, that is, to determine who used the Apple, how they used it and the characteristics of the games played. The findings tentatively support the observations of Levin and Cole. The microcomputer establishes an environment which supports, perhaps even requires, social interaction. The findings also lead to some questions regarding the relative importance of the factors identified by Malone. The games in Penny Arcade consisted of two white lines, approximately an inch long, which moved vertically on the screen, and a white "dot" which moved horizontally and diagonally on the screen. The screen was mostly black and sometimes contained obstacles composed of horizontal and vertical lines. This set-up is a relatively barren environment for fantasy. Other games, such as Sink the Ship, Depth Charge, Super Invaders, and Hangman, were relatively rich in fantasy features. Despite this disparity in fantasy features, Penny Arcade was the overwhelming favorite. The fantasy rich games were challenging, but only required one player. Could it be that social pressure, as well as the challenge of an opponent, is more compelling than the factor of fantasy? This question certainly deserves more study.

Two closely related limitations clearly affected the observations of the present study. Having only one Apple available established a situation which may have kept potential users away. The girls may have avoided the Apple primarily to avoid the aggressiveness of the boys using the Apple. Therefore, we cannot conclude that the girls in our lab were repelled by the machine. Also, by having only one machine and 48 hours of potential use there may not have been sufficient time for children to gain facility with the machine in more than just a rudimentary way. Thus, our findings must be considered in light of the environment.

The only clear generalization that may be drawn is that children's initial interaction style with the computer is a form of "messing about." Based on observations, this interaction was clearly positive. It may be recommended, then, that the initial step in planning for young children's use of computers should involve a period of computer play.

The current research leads to several new questions. Why were boys attracted to the center and not girls? Was this a function of the machine itself, the games available, competing centers, or lack of access? Why were there no younger children involved with the computer? The same factors in the previous question could be explored here. What periods of dormancy and exploration occur in using the computer? When observations ended, the subjects had stopped exploring the computer; would they emerge from this dormancy period, and if so, when? What behaviors can predict exploration and dormancy? What learnings are consolidated during the dormancy period?

These are but some of the questions to be considered in future research. The answers to these questions could be useful in preparing computer literacy programs for young children.

References

Instructional Use of Microcomputers Project. (1980). Joint Educational Management Research, University of Victoria, British Columbia.

Levin, J., & Cole, M. (1981, March). Untitled. In T.W. Malone & J. Levin (Eds.), *Microcomputers in education: Cognitive and social design principles*. Report of a conference sponsored by the Carnegie Corporation.

Loop, L. (1982, March). *CTUSA!—Autonomous learners in a formal library setting*. Paper presented at the annual meeting of the American Educational Research Association, New York, NY.

Malone, T.W. (1981, April). *What makes things fun to learn? A study of an intrinsically motivating instructional computer game*. Paper presented at the Annual Meeting of the American Educational Research Association, Los Angeles, CA.

Malone, T.W. (1980). *What makes things fun to learn? A study of intrinsically motivating computer games* (Technical Report CIS-7 SSL-80-11). Palo Alto, CA: Xerox Research Center.

Malone, T.W., & Levin, J. (Eds.). (1981). *Microcomputers in education: Cognitive and social design principles*. Report of a conference held March 12-14, 1981, sponsored by the Carnegie Institute.

Raskin, J. (1979). Students computers = learning. *Apple*, **1**, 22-23.

Ritchey, G.H., & Armstrong, E.L. (April, 1981). *Games children play*. Paper presented at the biannual meeting of the Society for Research in Child Development, Boston, MA.

Seidman, R.H. (1981, April). *The effects of learning a computer-programming language on the logical reasoning of school children*. Paper presented at the Annual Meeting of the American Educational Research Association, Los Angeles, CA.

Shalaway, L. (1980). Students' new classmates revolutionize education. *R and D Report*, **3**, 7-10.

APPENDIX

Microcomputer Observation Form

Observer: ——————————————————

MICRO COMPUTER OBSERVATION

1. Child's Name: ————————————   Date: ——————————

2. Time Entered Area: ——————————————

3. Time initiated interaction with Micro (If different from time entered area)

   ——————————————————————

4. If #3 different from #2, explain what the child was doing between the time he entered the area and the time he started using the Micro (tell *exactly* what child did):

5. List the games the child used on the micro and the length of time spent on each game.

6. How well did the child perform on each game? (List the name of the game and "score" or result achieved.)

7. Does the child appear to be using a consistent strategy in playing the game? (Describe in detail how the child is interacting with the micro.)

8. What kind of affect does the child display for each game? (*Describe in detail.*) Does he seem *excited* (animated of "oh boy," "yeah," etc.), *happy* (giggles, smiles, loose posture, verbalizations like "that's funny," "silly," etc.), *bored/uninterested* (attention wanders, expressionless—"blank eyes," verbalizations like "yuk," "oh brother," etc.)? If other than above, identify exactly what child does and characterize his behaviour.

9. Is the child playing alone or with others?

10. If with others, tell who.

11. If with others, describe their reaction *in detail.*

CHAPTER 6

Using the Computer for Early Childhood Screening, Writing Objectives, and Developing Local Norms/Records

CAROL MARDELL-CZUDNOWSKI
Northern Illinois University
and
DOROTHEA GOLDENBERG
Special Education Services Consultant
Lombard, Illinois

A computer program has been developed to assist users of DIAL-R, a widely used screening test, in the accurate scoring of young children's performance. In addition to print-out feedback for parents and teachers, the program generates suggested objectives for each child based on the child's chronological age and score for each of the 24 test items. Finally, the program stores up to 200 children's scores at each of the four age levels (2 year olds, 3 year olds, 4 year olds, 5 year olds) to enable administrators to analyze class, school, or district scores and develop local norms if desired.

KEY WORDS: DIAL-R, screening test, writing objectives, printout.

SCREENING young children and developing appropriate, individualized educational programs, regardless of whether the children's performance on the screening test yields scores of "potential problem," "O.K." or "potential advanced" is usually a time-consuming task. In addition, keeping track of children on multiple screenings during the preschool years, developing local norms instead of using national or state norms, or building a data base for school or district summary analyses can be both costly and difficult to achieve without massive paperwork. Now a computer program, DIAL-LOG, (Goldenberg, Mardell-Czudnowski, Abrams, and Bushong, 1986) has been developed for these purposes when the site uses DIAL-R. DIAL-R is a widely used screening test which is nationally normed and has acceptable reliability and validity (Mardell-Czudnowski & Goldenberg, 1983, 1984).

There are three parts to the computer program. Part A is designed to assist the screening coordinator. After quickly and accurately inputting the child's information directly from the DIAL-R scoresheet, Part A can perform the following functions:

* calculate accurate chronological age

* apply choice of cut-off points based on alternate distributions (1980 census, all white, all nonwhite) and total test score or subscores (Motor, Concepts, Language)

* display and print all pertinent child information including results based upon selected cut-offs (child report)

* print a hard copy report containing results and a developmental age analysis of each of the 24 individual scores of DIAL-R (detailed child report)

Figure 1 is an example of the child report on a three-year-old child. Figure 2 is an example of a detailed child report for the same child. School personnel could decide which reports to share with parents and teachers or place in school files.

Part B is the suggested activities program which works in conjunction with Part A and uses an analysis of the inputted results for a given child, producing a hard copy listing of suggested objectives for the teacher and/or parent in each of the three test areas (Motor, Concepts, Language). These objectives are specifically structured for the child based upon his or her age and responses to each item on DIAL-R. They enable staff to initiate appropriate objectives for a child with special needs, but they also direct the regular classroom teacher and/or the parent to the particular objectives which would be suitable for every child. Thus Part B provides a list of suggested objectives for any children whose DIAL-R item scores are below their chronological age. This list includes objectives starting at the age they actually achieved on the test item and continues through their present chronological age. In addition, it provides advanced objectives for any children whose scores indicate they are functioning at their chronological age on any tasks. Figure 3 shows the suggested objectives in the Language area for the child whose scores were shown in Figures 1 and 2.

Figure 1

DIAL-R Child Report

Child's Name:	Gladd, Ima
School Code:	B
Child's Sex:	Female
Child's C.A.:	3–6
Birth date:	March 16, 1982
Test date:	September, 20, 1985
Hearing score:	+ o.k.
Vision score:	− refer for additional observation
Motor score:	12
Results:	o.k.
Concepts score:	13
Results:	o.k.
Language score:	16
Results:	o.k.
DIAL-R score:	41
DIAL-R results:	o.k.
Motor observ:	2
Concepts observ:	1
Language observ:	2
Observ score:	5
Observ results:	refer for additional observation
Comments:	

Using the Language area as an example, this child scores '0' (below 2 years old) on Item 6—Classifying Foods so the suggested objectives range from age 2 through age 3 (her current age). On Item 7—Problem Solving, she scored '1' (2–0 to 2–11 years old). Since she is functioning as a two-year old, the objectives are designed to bring her to her current age level of three. On four items (1, 4, 5, and 8), she is functioning at age level so the program stated that fact and indicated the next level of objectives, in this case, the four-year-old level.

Finally, on two items, Giving Personal Data and Remembering, she scored beyond her current age level. Thus no activities were listed for these two tasks.

Figure 2

DIAL-R Detailed Child Report

Child's Name: Gladd, Ima
Child's C.A.:   3–6

Area	Scaled Score	Developmental Age
Motor		
1. Catching	0	Below 3 years old
2. Jump, Hop, and Skip	2	3–0—3–11 years old
3. Building	3	4–0—4–11 years old
4. Touching fingers	3	4–0—4–11 years old
5. Cutting	2	3–0—3–11 years old
6. Matching	1	2–0—2–11 years old
7. Copying	1	2–0—2–11 years old
8. Writing name	–	Task for older child
Concepts		
1. Naming colors	2	3–0—3–11 years old
2. Identify body parts	3	4–0—4–11 years old
3. Counting—rote	2	3–0—3–11 years old
4. Counting—meaningful	2	3–0—3–11 years old
5. Positioning	2	3–0—3–11 years old
6. Identifying concepts	2	3–0—3–11 years old
7. Naming letters	–	Task for older child
8. Sorting chips	–	Task for older child
Language		
1. Articulating	2	3–0—3–11 years old
2. Giving personal data	3	4–0—4–11 years old
3. Remembering	4	5–0—5–11 years old
4. Naming nouns	2	3–0—3–11 years old
5. Naming verbs	2	3–0—3–11 years old
6. Classifying foods	0	Below 2 year olds
7. Problem solving	1	2–0—2–11 years old
8. Sentence length	2	3–0—3–11 years old

Comments

Figure 3

Suggested Language Activities

Child's Name: Gladd, Ima
Child's C.A.:   3–6

Suggested Language activities can be initiated with continuous physical assist; intermittant physical assist; verbal and/or graphic assist, cue or model; and without assistance when requested.

1.   Articulation

   Age   *Suggested Activity*

           Functioning at present age level.

   4.   The child will repeat the sounds of N, NG, W, H, G, and vowel
           blends.

   4.   The child will initiate the sounds of N, NG, W, H, G, and vowel
           blends.

2.   Giving Personal Data

   Age   *Suggested Activity*

           Functioning above present age level.

3.   Remembering

   Age   *Suggested Activity*

           Functioning above present age level.

4.   Naming Nouns

   Age   *Suggested Activity*

           Functioning at present age level.

   4.   The child will point to pictures of less common objects such as an
           ambulance, jet, rocket, fire engine, typewriter, camera, or telescope
           when requested.

   4.   The child will label pictures of less common objects such as a camera,
           subway, elevator, and tractor when requested.

5.   Naming Verbs

    Age   *Suggested Activity*

               Fuctioning at present age level.

    4.   The child will point to pictures representing verb forms such as to comb, to write, and to go to the hospital.

    4.   The child will verbally label pictures representing less common verb forms such as to roll, to love, and to share.

6.   Classifying Foods

    Age   *Suggested Activity*

    2.   The child will categorize/classify two objects such as 2 edible items to fit the category of foods.

    3.   The child will categorize/classify four objects such as 4 edible items to fit the category of foods.

7.   Problem Solving

    Age   *Suggested Activity*

    3.   The child will describe a clear solution to simple problems such as what to do about hunger.

    3.   The child will describe a related solution to problems such as what to do about darkness or rainy weather.

8.   Sentence Length

    Age   *Suggested Activity*

               Fuctioning at present age level.

    4.   The child will initiate complete sentences of at least 5–6 words.

Part C is the record systems program which also works in conjunction with Part A and allows the user to build a file by storing the results of any designated child or children. Up to 200 children can be stored for each of the four age levels. This program can then process the file to generate the following information:

* an alphabetical listing, by child's last name, of child report results

* an alphabetical listing of children's results by school (up to 26 schools)

* charts of distributions by age levels according to the three area scores and the total scores

* percentiles, standard deviations, and standard errors of measurement for development of local norms and interpretation of data

While only 11% of all public elementary schools in the United States had computers in 1981, by 1983 62% had at least one microcomputer. It is estimated that by now, this percentage is up to 90–95%. Thus, it is conceivable that most sites serving preschool children will have access to the hardware to put this type of software into use. It is, therefore, relevant for such sites to know that their microcomputer can serve them in additional ways.

References

Goldenberg, D., Mardell-Czudnowski, C., Abrams, P. and Bushong, R. (1986) *DIAL-LOG*. Highland Park, IL: DIAL, Inc.

Mardell-Czudnowski, C. & Goldenberg, D. (1983). *DIAL-R* (Developmental Indicators for the Assessment of Learning-Revised) Manual. Edison, NJ: Childcraft Education Corporation.

Mardell-Czudnowski, C. & Goldenberg, D. (1984). Revision and restandardization of a preschool screening test: DIAL becomes DIAL-R. *Journal of the Division for Early Childhood*, **8**(2), 149–156.

CHAPTER 7

The DAISEY Data System: A Computerized System to Support Longitudinal Research

GARRETT K. MANDEVILLE

GAIL I. RAYMOND
and

LORIN W. ANDERSON
University of South Carolina

This paper describes a computerized System (DDCS) for collecting test scores and other data which will be useful in determining how children perform as they progress through the South Carolina public school system. Records from various statewide testing programs are linked by the use of student name, birthdate, gender and ethnicity to a data set reflecting experiences in a preschool program. The capability to capture these test data will facilitate the evaluation of the preschool program. Trial runs based on the children in the study who entered the first grade during the 1985–86 school year suggest that the DDCS has very low rates of mismatches and missed matches and that it is cost effective. Furthermore, it possesses other advantages relative to alternative methods of obtaining these data. Implications are drawn for research on child development and the evaluation of preschool intervention programs which are best addressed with longitudinal data bases.

KEY WORDS: Early childhood programs, program evaluation, child development, longitudinal studies, record-linking systems.

DURING the 1984–85 school year the Early Intervention for Academic Success project was pilot tested in six child development centers in South Carolina. The goal of this project is the prevention of learning problems adversely affecting school performance. Attainment of this goal is facilitated through diagnostic testing to determine student instructional needs in the areas of language, problem solving, and motor skills. The diagnostic and placement instruments were developed by project staff as were instructional materials in each of the three developmental areas. Serving disadvantaged students in the age range of 2 and one-half years to five years, the assessment and instructional materials are collectively referred to as the Developmental Assessment and Instruction for Success in Early Years (DAISEY) program.

Project staff were mindful of the need to evaluate the effects of the program and set up a quasi-experimental design for this purpose. The design called for two of the centers to be located in an urban area, two in a rural setting, and two in a small city. In each contextual setting, one center was designated to receive the full DAISEY treatment; in the other center, to serve as a control, only the assessment instruments, including posttests, were utilized.

One obvious source of evaluation evidence was the comparison of DAISEY and control children on the posttests. However, it was considered to be more important to assess the long range impact of the DAISEY treatment by observing the relative success of the two student groups once they had entered the public schools. Since *academic success* was the focus of DAISEY, the most important evidence was considered to be performance on achievement tests relevant to South Carolina school objectives. Fortunately, in 1980 the South Carolina General Assembly passed legislation mandating the development of statewide objectives in reading and mathematics and the annual statewide assessment of student achievement of these objectives. As a consequence the Basic Skills Assessment Program (BSAP) was implemented with criterion referenced tests administered in the spring of each year at grades, 1, 2, 3, 6, 8, and 10. These tests are relatively short, typically containing 36 reading items and 30 math items, six for each of the six reading and five mathematics objectives. Writing is assessed with a writing sample and only at the higher grades (i.e., 6, 8 and 10).

In addition to the BSAP, two other statewide testing programs are in operation. At the beginning of the school year the Comprehensive Skills Assessment Battery (CSAB) is individually administered to each first grader as a school readiness test. Furthermore, various levels of the Comprehensive Test of Basic Skills (CTBS) are given to all students who have completed grades 4, 5, 9 and 11. When these tests are administered, information on special programs (e.g., handicapped, gifted, Chapter I) in which the student may be enrolled, student descriptors (e.g., names, birthdates, gender, and ethnicity) and a school identifier are also coded onto the machine readable answer sheets. Project staff determined that these unobtrusive data, available at no additional expense (save the cost of accessing them), would be more than adequate for assessing the long term effects of the DAISEY intervention.

The initial objective of DAISEY staff was to obtain the test scores reflecting the first grade performance (CSAB and BSAP-1) of the children in the study. The two most obvious ways to obtain these scores would have been to contact the schools in which the children were enrolled or request the scores from the South Carolina Department of Education (DOE). Since only about 30 pilot children entered the first grade in the Fall of 1985, either approach would probably have succeeded. However, as more of the DAISEY and control children entered the public schools and as all children progressed from grade-to-grade, it is doubtful that either approach would have been completely successful.

The first approach would have been problematical for students who moved to another school and, in either case, the educational agencies involved might have been unwilling to allocate the necessary resources to accomplish the task. Furthermore, assuming that a process evaluation of the DAISEY pilot was positive, plans were in place to enter a larger implementation phase—to include approximately 20 centers serving more than 1000 children—during the 1986–87 school year. It was clear that it would have been exceedingly difficult and expensive to track such a large number of students, secure their test data, and enter these data for analysis; a more sophisticated and efficient system was needed. Because of the emphasis of this special issue, this paper will focus on the development and operation of a computerized system to capture these extant achievement data.

The remainder of this report will be presented in three sections. The first will provide a description of the data capture system developed by DAISEY staff. In the second section preliminary results on the performance of the system will be presented. A discussion of the implications for research and evaluation studies requiring longitudinal data sets containing test and other data for young children is provided in the concluding section.

DESCRIPTION OF THE DAISEY DATA CAPTURE SYSTEM (DDCS)

Background

The situation in which two data files are available with some records on each file relating to the same person or other object of interest (e.g., household) is often referred to as the "record linkage" problem. An

D

assumption is that a correctly specified unique identifier—such as a Social Security Number—is not available on all records since, if this were the case, the solution would be trivial. Rather, each file contains data on a number of descriptors such as name and birthdate, some of which may be incorrectly or partially recorded or missing. The objective is to use descriptive information common to both files to correctly link the records.

Many of the applied studies in this area have involved the medical field. Phillips, Bahn and Miyasaki (1962), for example, reported on the development of a data base of patient records while Cooley and Cox (1981) discussed a system for matching reports of recipients of medical care with those of providers. In another study, Freeman (1983) reported on a project to link Census of Agriculture records for 1976 and 1981.

In two recent papers (Jaro, 1984; Kelley, 1984) the authors have noted the advantages of what is called "blocking" the records to be matched. Briefly, blocking involves grouping the records on each file into mutually exclusive and exhaustive categories and restricting the search for matches to records which occur in the same blocks. The motivation to block according to Jaro (1984) is as follows:

> Obviously, if an entire file were searched for a match for each record, the probability of finding a true match would be highest since no records are excluded from consideration. However, the cost of such a process would be prohibitive. (p.599)

As an example, consider the situation in which the DAISEY data base (which will be referred to as file 1) contains 1000 students and that the state tape (file 2) contains 50,000 records. If each record in file 1 were compared to each record on file 2, fifty million comparisons would be required. This approach would be inefficient and would strain even a modern mainframe computer.

A more efficient strategy would be to use selected blocking variables to group the records on both files into a set of mutually exclusive and exhaustive categories and restrict the inter-file comparisons to records contained in the same categories. For example, suppose that 100 blocks were created and, for the sake of simplicity, assume that the records in both files were uniformly distributed across the blocks so that each block contains 10 file 1 records and 500 file 2 records. Within each block the number of comparisons would be 5000 and the total number would be reduced to one-half million (instead of 50 million). Although this is still a large amount of data processing, it is obviously more efficient in that only one percent as many comparisons are necessary.

In addition to increased efficiency, another advantage afforded by the blocking strategy may be increased accuracy. Consider that even in a relatively small state like South Carolina, the number of student records per grade (approximately 50,000) is quite large relative to the number to be matched, i.e., the number on the DAISEY data base. This increases the chances that students with the same or very similar descriptors as a DAISEY student may exist on the statewide data set, possibly resulting in an incorrect match.

Blocking Variables used in the DDCS

The DAISEY Data Capture System uses gender, ethnicity, birth month, and school district as blocking variables. Ethnicity codes other than black and white are combined into a third "other" category, to be taken in combination with the two gender and 12 birth month categories to produce 72 basic blocks.

School district information is used in the following way. South Carolina has 92 school districts which, for the purposes of the DDCS, were combined into 24 district groups based on size and geographic proximity. School districts were grouped in this fashion so that students who moved their residence but stayed within the same general geographic region of the state would likely remain in the same district grouping. This grouping variable in combination with the three discussed above produced a total of 1728 distinct blocks.

Processing Steps

The second general strategy which was incorporated into the DDCS is that it operates in discrete steps or "passes." The idea of a pass is based on the fact that correct matches vary on the ease with which they may be identified. To see this, let us consider how a human judge might go about the task. The judge could begin with a candidate DAISEY record and a listing of all file 2 records from the same school district-gender-ethnicity-birth month block. If the judge found a file 2 record from this block with the identical name and birthdate (including *month and day*), he or she would probably conclude that the match was a valid one. Such matches would be the easiest to identify since the blocking reduced the number of comparisons necessary and no judgement was actually required.

First pass The above is a rough description of the execution of the first pass of the DDCS. In actual fact, the computer does not make as many comparisons as might be inferred from the example above since both sets of records are ordered by birthday and name. Another difference was also introduced in an attempt to better simulate human judgement. A rational judge familiar with the format of the answer sheets would probably consider the names "BROWN RICHARD" and "BRQWN RICHARD" to represent the same child, assuming consistency on the other descriptors. The judge would be aware that coding errors such as the above are quite common because the "O" and "Q" columns of the name field on the answer sheets are in close proximity and obviously very similar in the visual sense. To simulate this type of decision making, a first-pass parameter allows for a match to be awarded if no more than a specified number of characters are in disagreement. This parameter is typically set to one. Experience has shown that generally, about 50 to 60 percent of the matches which are identified will be identified on this rather inexpensive (in terms of computer time) first pass. The main factors which affect this matching rate are the comparability of the name fields from the two files and, of course, the general quality of the data.

At the conclusion of the first pass, the records which have been matched are essentially removed from files 1 and 2. Although this is a simplification of the computer processing done in preparation for the second pass, it would be inappropriate to include the details in this paper. These residual files serve as the input files for pass 2.

Second Pass During the second pass, the residual records are processed along lines similar to those of pass 1 processing, except that the two names need not agree precisely (or, as is common, within one character). This approach was necessary for two reasons. First, student names and other descriptors are often inaccurate as they appear on the statewide tape files due to miscodings, omissions, or because the marks are too light to be correctly decoded by the optical reader. Second, the names students choose to use as their "first" names or that their teachers choose to call them tend to change from year to year. Thus John Robert Smith might be "SMITH JOHNNY" as far as his first grade teacher is concerned but may well be encoded as "SMITH ROBERT", "SMITH BOBBY", "SMITH J R", or some other permutation, in later years.

During this processing step, each file 1 record is compared to *all* file 2 records in the same block. During these comparisons a number of heuristic rules concerning the likelihood that the names on the two files represent the same child are applied and a "pseudo-probability" that the two records represent the same child is computed. The heuristic rules which have been operationalized in the algorithm were based on inspecting a large number of records and inferring the types of inconsistencies which arise.

If the pseudo-probability for the current file 2 record exceeds a program parameter (CRIT2), information on that record is retained while other file 2 records are considered. If a file 2 record with a higher pseudo-probability is found, it replaces the other as the best potential matching record. This process continues until all candidate file 2 records have been considered. At the end of pass 2 both files are again reduced by eliminating the matches which were identified.

Pass 2 processing, as described above, allows for one type of inconsistency among the student descriptors on the two files, namely, that the names may be quite different. All other information, however, is required to be consistent between the two files. Obviously, if processing were considered complete, DAISEY students for whom the blocking variables were miscoded on file 2 or who had moved to schools outside of their initial district grouping, would not be matched during the second pass. Third pass processing is designed to match these types of records.

Third pass During the third processing step two of the restrictions associated with pass 2 are modified. One is that the requirement that the two records be in the same district grouping is relaxed. The second is that the two records need not be in the same block based on the other three descriptors, i.e., gender, ethnicity and birth month. Rather, matches are considered if the records are consistent on only two of the descriptors. Because each file 2 record is a candidate match for a number of DAISEY records, it was not considered feasible to employ the approach of phase 2 processing in which each DAISEY record was compared to all eligible file 2 records before deciding which match was most likely valid. Thus, a more stringent criterion (CRIT3) regarding the comparability of the names from the two files was employed and when a match which attained or exceeded this criterion was identified, no further file 2 records were considered. In a sense, because the equivalence of the descriptor information was compromised, the two names were required to be more comparable than was true during the second pass.

Other Features of the DDCS

The above discussion has concentrated on the record-linking capability which is the heart of the DDCS. The matching is accomplished by a computer program of approximately 1200 statements written in the FORTRAN 77 language. The DDCS also includes pre- and post-processing job steps which utilize the Statistical Analysis System (SAS Institute, 1985) and the DAISEY data base is in fact a SAS data set. A convenient feature of the DDCS is that the user may identify the specific fields of file 2 for which data are to be retained. This is important because the statewide data files generally include item level data which are not of interest but which cause these records to be lengthy (often exceeding 1000 bytes). To enhance the flexibility of the system, the variables of interest are specified as input to the DDCS. The SAS variable names, their field specifications on file 2, and variable type (numeric or character) are read into the FORTRAN program which handles all data transfer activities and passes the appropriate information to the SAS post-processing step. Thus, at the conclusion of a job, the DAISEY data base is simply updated to include the new information.

RESULTS OF TWO TRIAL APPLICATIONS

When pilot students were enrolled in DAISEY, they were given a number of diagnostic and placement tests designed to prescribe the place within the curriculum at which instruction was to begin. At the same time, teachers determined the students' names, birthdates, gender, and ethnicity. At the completion of the year, this information, along with post assessment results, was incorporated into the DAISEY data base.

Although approximately 200 students were in the pilot study, only 33 were thought to have entered public first grade in the Fall of 1985, because the majority of the pilot study students were three- and four-years of age. As noted above, all first graders in South Carolina are individually tested by their teachers with the CSAB at the beginning of the school year. The Statewide tape file—which contained item data, raw and pass/fail scores on 12 CSAB readiness objectives, total CSAB raw score, and other information on the student—was made available by the DOE. DAISEY staff determined to retain information on 35 variables (25 related to the CSAB, the five descriptors needed by the DDCS, and five other variables such as eligibility for free or reduced price lunches) which accounted for 74 bytes of information (out of a total record length of 750 bytes). The matching results were as follows: 14 records were matched on the first pass, 17 more were matched on pass 2, and one other was matched on pass 3. The total of 32 out of 33 DAISEY records matched represents a success rate of 97 percent. A number of comments concerning details of these results are in order.

First, visual inspection of the names and other descriptors from the two files indicated that it was very likely that *no incorrect matches* were made. Second, it was subsequently determined that the unmatched child had moved to a neighboring state and, therefore, was not represented on the CSAB tape file. Thus, DAISEY staff are confident that all potential matches were correctly identified by the DDCS.

Concerning the matching rates on the various passes, fewer matches were identified on the first pass than would be expected based on earlier comments. The reason for this is that the name field on the CSAB answer sheet is restricted to a single field of only 15 characters so that the first name is often truncated (e.g., GLOVER JACQUELI). (The answer sheets for the other tests contain separate fields for the last and first name and the middle initial which total 28 characters.) Thus, fewer "exact" first pass matches are typically obtained when capturing CSAB data.

It should also be noted that as a trial computer run, file 2 data records were restricted to schools in the three districts these students were expected to attend (i.e., assuming that they had not moved). This restriction led to file 2 containing about 4000 records rather than the approximately 50,000 statewide. It had been anticipated that subsequent runs without this restriction would be necessary to identify any students who had moved in-state but this was not the case. On the technical side, processing time for the matching portion of the job was 16 sec. on an IBM 3081 mainframe processor; compilation of the FORTRAN program and pre-and post-processing increased the total cpu time to 37 sec.

At the end of the school year, all South Carolina first graders are tested with the BSAP. DAISEY staff requested information on 19 variables related to test performance and seven other variables dealing with whether the child was served by special programs such as Chapter I. Of the 400 byte records, 108 bytes of information were of interest. Of the 32 remaining records, 31 were matched (first pass–18; second pass–11; and third pass–2) with a total processing time of 36 sec. Although no information on the whereabouts of the missing record was available, the complete tape was searched for records with the same birthdate or names with character strings which were similar to the unmatched child and no reasonable matching case was identified. Again, inspection indicated a strong likelihood that all 31 matches were correct. Therefore, it appears that in both trial applications the DDCS accurately identified *all* of the possible matches.

DISCUSSION

It is not anticipated that the apparent 100 percent matching accuracy of the DDCS will be replicated as more DAISEY students enter the public schools. However, large scale applications of the matching algorithm to other problems have yielded very low rates of incorrect matches and missed matches. For example a state-level analysis to match all CSAB and BSAP-1 records led to 48,161 (92·9 percent) of the 51,841 BSAP-1 records being matched. Visual inspection led to the identification and elimination of seven matches which were clearly incorrect (four involved two mismatched sets of twins). In addition, 292 computer matches, the validity of which was quite ambiguous, were identified. In most of these cases, the descriptors were consistent but the name field was limited to last name only on one file. Although the majority were probably correct, no easy method of verification was available. If all 299 are considered as erroneous matches, the mismatch rate is only about ·6 percent. This same visual editing also uncovered 223 likely missed matches which corresponds to an error rate of less than ·5 percent.

There have been a number of attempts to measure the long-range effectiveness of child development programs and early intervention strategies. In 1974, Bronfenbrenner, in his now famous monograph, focussed attention on the question of the long-range efficacy of early intervention. More recently other researchers have endeavored to examine the longitudinal effects of such programs on poor children, at risk children, and handicapped children (for reviews see Beller, 1979; Brown, 1978; Clark-Stewart & Fein, 1983; Lazar & Darlington, 1982). Even though there have been a number of studies on the issue, there is still doubt as to the effectiveness of early intervention. One reason for the inconclusive nature of these findings is that researchers concerned with the long-term development of young children have traditionally been hamstrung by the difficulty of, and cost involved in, the conduct of longitudinal studies. As a consequence, short-term, cross-sectional data have been used as indicators of the *likelihood* that long-term benefits of the program will accrue. Similarly, quasi-longitudinal data (typically involving students at different grade levels who are believed to be sufficiently similar to one another to allow meaningful comparisons) have been a convenient substitute for true longitudinal studies. Using these data, then, the science of longitudinal tracking has been preempted by the arts of extrapolation and persuasion.

The DAISEY Data Capture System is an accurate, cost-effective approach to longitudinal tracking which will support studies of long-term child development as well as studies of the impact of early intervention on school success. The system permits the matching of more than 90 percent of students included in chronologically-distinct data sets with an error rate of less than one percent. The system post-development cost was about 30 cents per student per computer run. This figure is far less than what could be expected if matching and retrieval of student data were done "by hand."

In many ways, then, the DDCS permits more effective and efficient study of a number of questions and issues in the field of early childhood education and child development. Through such study, early identification and appropriate intervention can hopefully contribute to the positive cognitive development and school success for ever-increasing numbers of children in our society.

References

Beller, E.K. (1979). Early intervention programs. In J.D. Osofsky (Ed.), *Handbook of infant development* (pp. 852–894). New York: Wiley.

Bronfenbrenner, U. (1974). *Is early intervention effective?* Washington, DC: Office of Human Development.

Brown, B. (1978). *Found: Long-term gains from early intervention.* Boulder, CO: Westview Press.

Clark-Stewart, K.A. and G.C. Fein (1983). Early childhood programs. In M.M. Haith and J.J. Campos (Eds.), *Infancy and developmental psychology* (pp. 917–1000). New York: Wiley

Cooley, P. and B. Cox (1981). An automated procedure for matching record check and household-reported health care data. *Proceedings of the Social Statistics Section*, American Statistical Association, 418–423.

Freeman, R.W. (1983). 1981 to 1986 census of agriculture record linkage. *Proceedings of the Bureau of Economic Statistics Section*, American Statistical Association, 91–99.

Jaro, M. (1984). Record linkage research and the calibration of record linkage algorithms. *Proceedings of the Social Statistics Section*, American Statistical Association, 599–601.

Kelley, R.P. (1984). Blocking considerations for record linkage under conditions of uncertainty. *Proceedings of the Social Statistics Section*, American Statistical Association, 602–609.

Lazar, I. and R. Darlington (Eds.). (1982). Lasting effects of early education: A report from the Consortium for Longitudinal Studies. *Monographs of the Society for Research in Child Development*, **47**,(2–3, Serial No. 195).

Phillips, W., A.K. Bahn and M. Miyasaki (1962). Person-matching by electronic methods. *Communications of the Association of Computing Machinery*, **5**, 404–407.

SAS user's guide: Basics (Version 5 Edition). (1985). Cary, NC: The SAS Institute.

CHAPTER 8

Computers and cognitive development: A preliminary statement

JOHN W. MURPHY
University of Miami
and
JOHN T. PARDECK
Southeast Missouri State University

TECHNOLOGY is currently proliferating throughout society at an unprecedented rate, as computers are introduced into the home, farm, factory, and classroom. In fact, Jacques Ellul (1964, pp. 127–128) contends that today's world represents a "technological civilization". This does not mean simply that machines have come to dominate society, but, more importantly, that "technological rationality" has infiltrated every facet of social life. Yet most often technology is equated with machinery, thereby obscuring the impact of this style of reasoning (Murphy and Pardeck, 1985a). Such an oversight is particularly problematic for education, since computerized instruction is now included in a child's curriculum as early as possible.

Central to this discussion is the argument that technology is not just machinery. Instead, technology is sustained by a particular form of logic or reason that affects how persons view both themselves and their environment. And although computers are playing an ever increasing role in children's education, little time has been devoted to discussing the possible influence of technological rationality on their cognitive development. Actually, when the impact of educational technology has been examined, most often the focus of attention has been the changes in classroom structure brought about by technological innovations (Broughton, 1985). Because the "social imagery" that accompanies computerized learning is not given serious attention, the ways in which computers may be shaping students' thought processes have not been addressed. Accordingly, the aim of this paper is to (1) outline the key tenets of technological rationality and (2) demonstrate how they suggest the world should be conceptualized.

Modern theorists are beginning to recognize that computers do not operate solely on the basis of technical knowledge, and thus are not "value-free". In order for computer operations to make sense, they must be accompanied by specific philosophical assumptions that are acknowledged to be valid. These beliefs, in other words, serve as a referent for interpreting the data that are entered into a computer, while also dictating the significance of the logic that is indigenous to computerization. Marvin Minsky (1981), for example, has argued that these assumptions constitute a "frame" for diagnosing a typical situation. Because any datum is infinitely complex, a particular set of criteria must be invoked to differenciate relevant from irrelevant information. In a sense, these principles define reality in a unique manner and, thus, construct what is called a "micro-world" (Dreyfus, 1979). Computers, accordingly, actively shape both their users and the information they analyze, due to the influence of the procedural tenets that are central to data processing.

What this means is that computers establish their own environment for learning, a sort of "computer culture" (Mickunas, 1985). Nonetheless, what are the fundamental characteristics of the technological "world-view"? First, all phenomena are treated as matter, or inert objects. Second, an abstract calculus is adopted to identify anything that is known, since mathematics is treated as most appropriate for measuring the dimensions of matter. And third, the laws of physics are understood to determine the course of events and behavior. Taken together, these three axioms form the cornerstone of technological rationality and are indispensible for computerization. This form of reasoning is valued because knowledge is allegedly purged of interpretation, thereby revealing scientific or objective data. Furthermore, because technological rationality is thought to represent the paragon of reason, other modes of assessing information are diminished in importance. As a result, the cognitive schemes utilized by children can easily be "inferiorized", because they do not necessarily think scientifically (Adam, 1978, p. 6). When compared to a computer, simply put, a child appears to be capricious.

Because of the emphasis placed on objective data by the proponents of the Information Age, the whimsicalness exhibited by children while they learn is not always appreciated. Yet when rationality is juxtaposed to irrationality in this way, primacy is usually given to the former. This is because reason is touted to provide the only access to truth. And because computers are thoroughly rational, children's logic appears to be replete with error by comparison. Accordingly the stage is set for the scheme used by children to assess information to be dismissed as unreliable, since the resulting knowledge is believed to be idiosyncratic. Children can thus be convinced readily that their thought processes should be replaced by those indigenous to computerization.

Computers do not serve simply as a tool to solve problems, but, in a manner of speaking, participate in defining what it means for something to be problematic. Because only certain types of information are deemed to be valid, a limited data base is available for evaluating a situation. This is not a version of technological determinism, since technology does not *cause* persons to do anything. The conditions are merely established whereby a particular rendition of knowledge is given a seignorial status, thus encouraging persons to develop a specific approach to classifying data. Additionally, this form of cognition is invulnerable to critique, for it is assumed to be synonymous with rational thinking. Understood in this way, the social imagery that is advanced by technological rationality is equated with reality and goes unquestioned (Murphy and Pardeck, 1985b). Yet this conception of reality is predicated on assumptions that have practical consequences for the activities of thinking and valuation.

The question remains, however, how is information objectified through computerization, so that it appears to be unaffected by persons' cognitive operations? In order for data to be processed by a computer they must be treated as "bits" of information (Weizenbaum, 1976, pp. 39–72). For only in this way can knowledge be made to conform to the explicit conceptual dignits used by computers to classify input. What this means is that a datum cannot have a symbolic identity, but only one derived from its empirical or objective traits. Otherwise, information would be ambiguous and not readily adaptable to the logical or "address" space that is presupposed by computerization (Bolter, 1984, pp. 83–90). Knowledge, in other words, must be catalogued in a binary manner, so that no piece of information can have a variety of interpretations. Only findings that can be pigeonholed neatly are useful, since they do not challenge the precision necessary for computers to analyze data rapidly. Nothing causes more confusion in a highly formalized system than facts with vague parameters.

In less philosophical language, data must be stripped of their metaphorical sense and transformed into objects. Such material is easily coded, i.e., given an explicit identity, and assigned a proper storage space. According to the mandates imposed by technological rationality, computerization materializes information. Moreover, quantitative procedures are usually employed to codify data, as mathematics is considered to be rigorous and precise. Knowledge is thus envisioned to have empirical properties that can be indexed numerically, without any loss of meaning. Yet these bits of information are basically unorganized and meaningless until a program, operating behind the scenes, so to speak, provides the entire system with direction. At this juncture, the illusion is created that knowledge is divorced from the contingencies associated with daily life, because computerized data inhabit a world that is purely logical and unaffected by interpretation. The computer culture is not ordered poetically, but is comprised of abstract units that are mechanically regulated (Bachelard, 1964, pp. 38–73).

When children are exposed to this process, particularly in a context which designates technological rationality to epitomize reason, their cognitive activities can easily be made to conform to the technical strictures imposed by computer logic. Félix Guattari (1984, pp. 111–119), for instance, suggests that the interaction that occurs between technological rationality and humans is a form of terrorism, as they are intimidated into abandoning their beliefs because subjectivity becomes an impediment to the acquisition of truth. The modality of cognition associated with technological rationality is traditionally known as naive realism (Neisser, 1976, pp. 13–32). By this is meant that the world is portrayed as unquestionably real, and therefore does not need to be supplemented by interpretation for it to have significance. Existence, in short, operates according to rules that cannot be denied, despite how they are perceived.

Throughout the educational process this realism is manifested in various ways. First, facts are encountered in such a manner that they are associated inadvertently with objective things. As

Hubert Dreyfus (1972, pp. 235–255) argues, facts have no "body" when they are articulated within the parameters specified by computerization. The corporeal nature they are lacking originates from the human element of knowledge acquisition, or interpretation. Learning, therefore, becomes nothing more than gaining expertise at classifying pieces of data properly and expediciously. Facts are simply located, placed in a "workspace" in a computer, and organized in a systematic way.

Second, this treatment of facts means that education is largely an activity whereby information is manipulated, although sophisticated instructions are followed. In a sense, computerized education allows children ample opportunity to "message" their data, as the programs and sub-routines that are currently available are almost unlimited. Nonetheless, this strategy for data analysis obscures the judgements that lend credence to certain information. Little is said about the factor of interpretation that serves to select data and establishes the social context for their use. What is mostly emphasized, instead, is the refinement of technique, so that knowledge can be increasingly formalized.

Third, although conceived to be quite intricate, the world is purged of all wonder. According to the early Greeks, education begins with wonderment, or when the elusive character of knowledge is recognized. Enthusiasm is thus introduced into learning, because knowledge is not something obtrusive and static (Murphy, forthcoming: a). Consequently the world is not considered to be ultimately real, but a phenomenon that must be evaluated for its importance to be revealed. The human element is vital to knowledge acquisition, since only personal judgements differentiate reality from illusion. Nonetheless, during computerized learning this determination is made in terms of technical criteria, as opposed to volition. What this accomplishes is the systematic removal of passion from students.

And fourth, imagination or creativity is diminished throughout the learning process. This is because subjectivity is ubiquitous to these activities, and thus they can only impair a person's perception of the truth. Due to the stress placed on analytical skills, children are cajoled into adopting a cognitive style that is passive and not very imaginative. The world can be dissected and reassembled effectively, yet the price paid for these abilities is quite dear. Specifically, students are taught how to mimic instructions without understanding their rationale, other than how they are technically justified.

Most important is that technology is not value-free, but subtly socializes its users. The logic that underpins computerization circumscribes the limits of valid data, and specifies the range of legitimate analysis. In terms of the social world, a key implication is that the human element of learning is unimportant, or at least a hindrance to the acquisition of unbiased knowledge. Thus society becomes a fixed structure which needs only periodic adjustment to function properly. Those who are considered to be intelligent are most adept at diagnosing a malfunction and prescribing a remedy. If this can be called creativity, at best it is convergent in nature. This increasing rationalization of cognition narrows the scope of problems and their possible solutions. In a word, reflexive thinking is undermined, for the cognitive flexibility necessary for this demarché is not available.

An absence of reflexive analysis, or self-criticism, is the hallmark of what is nowadays referred to as the "bureaucratic personality" (Merton, 1952). This syndrome includes traits such as an intolerance of ambiguity, excessive stereotyping, and the ritualization of role behavior. Although usually they are though to be spawned by a particular social system, through the imposition of a rigid organizational structure, such characteristics can also be produced by a strategy for instilling knowledge.

If educators are not careful, an approach to learning that is extolled as capable of expanding the horizons of the mind may in fact stifle the imagination and subvert critical thinking. For the "micro-world" of the computer is very influential.

Because of the stress placed on efficiency cognition is equated with data processing, as opposed to the *generation* of knowledge. Perceptual acuity becomes an index of learning, as the misclassification of data cannot be tolerated. Translated into social action, this suggests that logistical refinements are sufficient to sustain order among persons. What this overlooks is the toleration that individuals in a pluralistic society must have for one another, particularly in terms of how they interpret each other's behavior. Order does not occur simply because someone can calculate the most technically efficient method for structuring the social system. Instead, the polity is a product of interpersonal dialogue, whereby claimants learn to negotiate a mutually acceptable mode of interacting. The early Greeks, in fact, reorganized this activity to be at the heart of a non-repressive society (Borgmann, 1984, pp. 78–101). Today, however, this idea may be jeopardized, if technological machinations are tacitly suggested to be sufficient to solve any crisis. Political action is not a technical undertaking, but one based on the *recognition of differences* (Luhmann, 1982, pp. 353–355). Computerization may cause this art of dialogue to atrophy, by unduly formalizing students' cognitive processes. For without self-reflection and interpretation non-coercive dialogue among persons is impossible. If bureaucracy is to be reduced in society, as many politicians desire, then rigid cognitive styles must not be fostered.

The point of this paper is not to attribute every social problem to the introduction of computers into the classroom, but to suggest ways in which this technology may alter children's perception of themselves, others, and their environment. When

examining the impact of educational technology this type of
analysis is mostly overlooked, as the focus of attention is the
logistical changes inaugurated in education by computers
(Murphy, forthcoming: b). This discussion addresses the theoretical tenets of technology, along with some of their more relevant
social implications. Most important is that computerized learning establishes the conditions for the development of a particular
cognitive style on the part of students, one which may prove to
be quite stifling socially. And without understanding how computerization affects a child's social-cognitive growth, the long-
term effects of computerized learning cannot be anticipated and
corrected.

References

Adam, B.D. (1978). *The Survival of Domination*, New York: Elsevier.

Bachelard, G. (1964). *The Poetics of Space*, New York: The Orion Press.

Bolter, J.D. (1984). *Turing's Man: Western Culture in the Computer Age*, Chapel
    Hill: University of North Carolina Press.

Borgmann, A. (1984). *Technology and the Character of Contemporary Life*,
    Chicago: University of Chicago Press.

Broughton, J.M. (1985). The Surrender of Control: Computer Literacy as
    Political Socialization of the Child. In D. Sloan (Ed.), *The Computer in
    Education: A Critical Perspective* (pp. 102–122), New York: Columbia
    University Press.

Dreyfus, H.L. (1979). A Framework for Misrepresenting Knowledge. In M.
    Ringle (Ed.), *Philosophical Perspectives in Artificial Intelligence* (pp.124–136),
    Atlantic Highlands, NJ: Humanities Press.

Dreyfus, H.L. (1972). *What Computers Can't Do*, New York: Harper and Row.

Ellul, J. (1964). *The Technological Society*, New York: Random House.

Guattari, F. (1984). *Molecular Revolution: Psychiatry and Politics*, New York:
    Penguin Books.

Luhmann, N. (1982). *The Differentiation of Society*, New York: Columbia
    University Press.

Mickunas, A. (1984). The Essence of the Technological World. In L. Embree
    (Ed.), *Essays in Memory of Aron Gurwitsch* (pp. 98–116), Washington,
    D.C.: University Press of America.

Minsky, M. (1981). A Framework for Representing Knowledge. In J. Haugeland (Ed.), *Mind Design* (pp. 95–128), Montgomery, VT: Bradford Books.

Murphy, J.W. (forthcoming: a)   Computer Mediated Education: A Critique, *Pedagogy and Phenomenology*.

Murphy, J.W. (forthcoming: b).   Humanizing the Use of Technology in Education: A Re-examination, *International Review of Education*.

Murphy, J.W. and Pardeck, J.T. (1985a).   The Technological World-View and the Responsible Use of Computers in the Classroom, *Journal of Education*, **167**(2): 98–108.

Murphy, J.W. and Pardeck, J.T. (1985b).   Social Imagery, Rules of Order, and Therapy, *Family Therapy*, **12**(2): 97–114.

Merton, R.K. (1952).   Bureaucratic Structure and Personality. In R.K. Merton, A.P. Gray, B. Hockey, and H.C. Selvin (Eds.), *Readings in Bureaucracy* (pp. 361–371), New York: The Free Press.

Neisser, U. (1976).   *Cognition and Reality*, San Francisco: W.H. Freeman.

Weizenbaum, J. (1976).   *Computer Power and Human Reason*, San Francisco: W.H. Freeman.

CHAPTER 9

A Critical Look at Children and Microcomputers: Some Phenomenological Observations

LARRY W. KREUGER

HOWARD KARGER
and
KATHY BARWICK
Missouri University

This paper focuses on a critical analysis of computer technology through the phenomenological approach. The psychological and sociological effects of introducing children to computers are discussed, including the impact that computers have on the child's sense of time and the potential negative effect computers have on the play of children. The article concludes that the trend toward computer technology in the classroom cannot be turned back; however, it is critical that educators understand the long term consequences of computer technology on children and attempt to insure that this technology does not become an agent of repression.

KEY WORDS: Computers and time, computers and play, and phenomenology.

THE PURPOSE of this article is to provide a phenomenological analysis of the relationship between children and microcomputers. As part of that examination, the article will probe the negative psychological and sociological effects of introducing young children to computers including: perceptual shifts in the child's sense of time; the effect of mechanistic interactions between children and computers; dangers of involving a non-critical and passive acceptance of technology; and the commodification of play.

SOME BASIC PERCEPTS OF PHENOMENOLOGY

This paper employs phenomenological analysis to explore several features and possible consequences of the encounter between children and microcomputers. A phenomenological investigation of children and microcomputers presents an interesting methodological problem; namely, neither children nor microcomputers are readily available for analysis. Both children and microcomputers provide to phenomenological investigators only an outer horizon or shell from which understandings about various inner workings must be inferred. Available for analysis are only small glimpses of child microcomputer encounters which can be culled from a handful of observable projects. Both child and machine—one presumably driven by affective conditions and the other propelled by purely linear, cognitive-like manipulations—present to the researcher a nearly impenetrable social and psychological opacity.

Should one attempt an incursion in to the finite province of child-encountering-computer by reconstructing reality based upon one's own experiences, the project necessarily fails because the orignal polythetic encounter between the child and the machine remains forever beyond the horizon of the life-world of adults. Moreover, the lack of availability in our own childhood of analogous technology similar to microcomputers, further limits our ability to reconstruct parallel experiences. It is with this caveat that the authors begin the analysis.

Phenomenological investigation has its origins in the writings of Edmond Husserl. American writers including Alfred Schutz, George Psathas, Peter Berger and Thomas Luckman, further developed phenomenology within the purview of social science theory (Husserl, 1931; Schutz, 1966; Spiegelberg, 1971; Berger and Luckman, 1967; Wolff, 1978; Psathas, 1973).

Of special importance is the work of Alfred Schutz, who attempted to unify many of the principles of Husserl with social science theory, and in particular, with the social theory of Max Weber. Schutz's analysis of interpersonal encounters, and his investigation of the solitary individual's relation to larger society, provide the foundation for this analysis. (Schutz, 1966).

The phenomenology of Schutz focuses on the individual as a "knowing mind" which confronts the physical and social environment with varying degrees of attentiveness. Phenomenology begins with an examination of the invariant features of those objects which come to the individual's conscious attention, as if they were matters of insight or intuition. (Schutz, 1966)

Phenomenological analysis begins with an examination of what enters in the conscious mind when the world is encountered "head on;" that is, when the individual examines objects from the external world as they "appear" in one's conscious mind. Phenomenological analysis does not generate traditionally empirical answers to such questions as may be raised by an examination of "appearances," but rather suggests lines of inquiry for assessing the solitary individual's situation relative to larger spheres of life. (Schutz, 1966).

One problem with phenomenological analysis is that it carries with it the burden of a "tribal" language, thus requiring either elaborate explanations, definitions, references to orignal authors or a compromise. In this paper the authors have chosen to compromise phenomenological analysis; that is, we have modified phenomenology to include a critical theory perspective.

THE LITERATURE OF MICROCOMPUTERS AND CHILDREN

Most of the current research studies examine the interaction of children and microcomputers in the context of schools. While useful, these studies contain no clear evidence regarding the positive or negative effects of microcomputers on children. In a study of preschools equipped with computers, Klinzing (1985) maintains that computers seem to encourage both cooperative and independent play. A study by Williams, Beeson, and Spillers (1985) found that the computer is similar to other activities found in a preschool; some students love it, others have little interest. Moreover, according to Williams et al., when preschool children were given a choice between puzzles/bristle blocks and computers, they spent more time playing with the former. Colker (1983) maintains that there is no more inherent conflict in providing preschool children with computers than in providing them with conventional playthings. Sheingold (1984) believes that the symbolic nature of the microcomputer does not make it inappropriate for use by young children. The microcomputer can, she believes, provide cognitive support as a means for reflecting on other activities and better understanding other media, as well as help children take a broader view of the computer as an important piece ot technology.

The endorsement of computers for preschool children is not universally shared. Abt (1980) fears that the television and computer age has a potential to lead to social isolation and withdrawal, ultimately resulting in psychosis. Heller and Martin (1982) fear that children may choose to interact with machines rather than people. And Barnes and Hill (1983) believe that children are likely to experience problems in social behaviour if computers limit their social interaction. If these studies inform us of anything, it is of our relative ignorance regarding either the positive or negative effects of computers on children. Within this context the following analysis is not intended as a finished product, but as a series of questions to be asked of those crusaders who frantically demand we immerse children in the presumed technological world of the future.

PSYCHOLOGICAL EFFECTS OF COMPUTERS ON CHILDREN

The outcome of repeated and sustained contacts between children and computers involve both the medium (the process of relaying the data) and the implicit—and often explicit—message inherent in the software. Possible effects of computers on children must therefore be seen as a phenomena involving a complex weave of both form and content messages. The dynamic interaction between form and content makes the microcomputer a formidable social milestone.

One of the most obvious changes experienced by computer users is the shifting arrangement of time. As users become more familiar with computers they begin to wonder about its speed. The time which they have available to use when encountering a microcomputer appears accelerated, with the machine performing tasks much more rapidly than they can comprehend. There is no simultaneity to this engagement. While the machine requires input and responds with virtually simultaneous visual and auditory cues, its computational capability far exceeds any parallel human computational processes.

In contradistinction to computers, children must live with the limitations of the "processing speed" of their own stream of consciousness. Children have experiences where adults speak in phrases they cannot comprehend. Adults sometimes speak so rapidly that children cannot interpret their intentions without asking them to slow down. While adults will often slow their tempo, children find that they cannot slow down their microcomputer—it proceeds precisely and inexorably at a speed which rarely changes pace.

Events occur in the child's world of everyday life against a backdrop or horizon which is perceived as a stable environment. They witness numerous "speedy" events, (i.e. a speeding car, bolt of lightning etc.) but such events always occur in their world of everyday life relative to a tangible background which rarely moves. Microcomputer events, on the other hand, occur against a darkened background. It seems as if nightfall is forever behind events on the screen. What users see on the screen is an artificially lighted activity which appears to move very rapidly against an opaque horizon. Microcomputer events thus seem to happen at nearly the speed of light.

The rapid speed of the microcomputer pales in contrast to the sluggishness of everyday events. In contrast, instructions given by teachers seems boring and interminable. Occurring at a slower pace than machine interaction, human association may appear lackluster. Even television with its rapid fire editing and quick pace seems tedious when compared to the pace of video games. As Brod (1984) suggests, time accelerates for video game players while patience becomes more easily exhusted.

Young children need to learn to control their impulses and suppress their desire for instant gratification. Computer encounters, especially video games, appeal to instant gratification and compulsive thinking. The electronic medium responds instantly, and after the system is learned, it provides little real frustration. Thus, while the intensity of the electronics provides constant stimulation at an almost relentless tempo, it also helps shorten the already brief attention span of children. As the sensory threshold for stimulation increases, everyday life events become more monotonous.

Computers defy the rules of everyday life in other ways. In the normal world of everyday life, children find they can negotiate their way around environmental obstacles using inductive and deductive logic in combination with what seems to be spontaneous bursts of insight. For the most part, children do not need to pay attention either to logical processes or to their intuition. The "dance" of activity in everyday life is not one they encounter via a programmed "execution."

When children encounter microcomputers they find themselves a solitary figure engaged in activities using objects and relations which do not exist in the world of everyday life. For example, within a microcomputersubprovince of meaning they can remake, alter or otherwise strike out features of that subprovince without affecting the outer world. Moreover, there is little analogy in the world of everyday life which refers to or points toward microcomputer experience. As a computer user, the child is caught up in a subprovince of meaning which can only have meaning to those who have visited a similar province. Other visitors and the child come to share a special language which is not easily translatable into the ordinary vernacular of everyday life.

The interaction between children and computers is a mechanistic one. Although software programs try to emulate human encouragement (e.g. Good Job,! That's the Right Answer, and so forth) they do so in a stilted machine sense. Realizing that the development of children involves both the cognitive and emotional realms, yet incapable of providing real emotional feedback, programmers substitute proxy human responses, which in the end, prove more confusing and dishonest to the child. Despite their messages of encouragement, computers do not possess the capacity to care whether Sally or Johnny got the answer right. Nevertheless, programmers craft software intended to give the illusion of warmth and concern. For many young children confused about the line between fantasy and reality, this misrepresentation only obfuscates what is real and true.

The mechanistic interaction between children and computers involve other realms. In a society where human bonds are being replaced by electronic association, and knowledge is seen as a commodity that must be rationalized and managed, the needs of children for personal attention becomes an irritant. Given the escalating costs of education, schools look with hopefulness to educational methodologies that are less expensive and therefore less labor intensive. Computer based educational methodologies meet those needs.

In the world of everyday life, children find they enjoy the spontaneity of other people and are sometimes surprised by their words or deeds of others. Their experience in the world of everyday life has an intersubjective element; that is, children find their own understanding of events in the world are colored by the interpretations made by others. They grow older with others, and the expressivity of other people continuously reminds the child of his or her status as a member of a community of other knowing minds. Children are aided by the language available to them in everyday life, which carries along with it a set of meanings they employ to understand themselves in relation to others. In short, children experience the world as an inter-connected series of embedded relationships.

Computer encounters, on the other hand, are characterized by "thought in isolation." In time, some users find they become so absorbed in microcomputer encounters, they can return to the world of everyday life only with some effort. Boulter (1984) describes the isolation of a computer's actions:

> embodied, but it's embodiment remains curiously separated from the rest of the physical world . . . isolated in the way that all mathematical or logical thought is isolated: it allows for no possibility of immediate union between two thinkers. (p. 78).

Microcomputer encounters are solitary endeavors, which for the most part, presume little or no communication with other human beings. Since computer use requires a dyadic interaction, opportunities for socializing with others is curtailed. This reduction of interaction may help to diminish social development skills; especially, for the introverted child. The seductive isolation offered by computer use may well increases the alienation and loneliness of the introverted youngster.

Schneider and Schneider (1984) maintain that computers can attract children who have difficulty in social interaction. These socially inept children enjoy the lack of interpersonal complications offered by a computer; since unlike human relationships, computers are predictable, do not threaten personal rejection, demand no human commitment, are easy to get along with (if you know the rules), and can never make demands. This may lead the lonely child to personalize the machine's relationship to him or her. The child therefore begins to experience the machine as more subjective over time, and it's repetitive and even dull presentation of reliable, predictable content, becomes a province which they escape to. Such children find themselves no longer a solitary figure, and they encounter their microcomputer as a machine filled with predictable, stable and even friendly responses. For the child frightened by human intimacy, computers provide a low risk area of satisfaction—a seduction that will become more tempting with the advent of talking computers.

In the mind of the child (as well as for many adults) the computer is seen as an undisputed authority figure which provides the omniscient voice of truth. Within this power configuration the child has no opportunity for discussion or disagreement, and no chance to ask how, where, when and why the program came to possess the information. In the black box of the computer there is a monopoly where little room exists for questions, and where inquisitiveness or discussion which might breed critical thought is prohibited by the medium. Seltzer and Karger (1974) maintain that:

> This system operates to prevent genuine learning from developing; it does not allow for a process where ideas can be conceptualized and tested, where hypotheses can be scrutinized and replaced if need be, where new thoughts can evolve, and where all of these things can be talked about among living, breathing, and thinking human beings. Instead, the learning situation is one wherein absolute truths are taught, questions are not answered, discussions are denied, and the exchange of ideas between human beings is prevented. (p. 14)

What is learned, then, is passivity and alienation from oneself and others, and that the most fruitful relationships with people will be as passive and impersonal as the solitary interaction with the computer. The child learns that the messages and commands broadcast through electronic media are more valid than the speech and gestures of the less-than-perfect human beings. Moreover, the child comes to understand that the voice of technology possesses a monopoly on truth and values: the program determines the right and wrong answer. This is only a short step to the kind of mind pacification which says that more bombs produce more security, "misinformation" is not lying, and war is peace.

Backed by the theoretical formulations of a cadre of cognitive psychologists, many educators are beginning to perceive the human brain as a computer (Brod, 1984). This model of human cybernetics stresses the value of speed, efficiency, reliability, and uniformity. While the cybernetic model clearly prescribes the role of teaching and learning, it doesn't adequately address creativity, humanism, and emotional affect. When brains are seen as computers, emotions become an irritating stumbling block to true learning.

COMPUTER AGE VALUES AND THE COMMODIFICATION OF PLAY

The frenzied attempt to introduce children to computers did not happen in a haphazard fashion: it was part of an overall strategy endorsed by computer corporations, the state, and an upwardly mobile middle class. Computers are a lucrative business.

The introduction of children to computers does not merely represent good short term business sense. Acquainting children with computers in the present assures a readily available non-techno-phobic consumer force prepared to buy the newest technological appurtenances of the future. More importantly, these computer suckled children will learn to embrace new technological achievements without a critical appraisal as to their social ramifications and their impact on the quality of life. The debate will range over the technical aspects of the new technology rather than on its social implications, and whatever voices of resistance persist will be silenced by the indifference of the crowd.

The covert message lodged within the membrane of the new technology provides children with a technocratic perspective on life: a perspective which sees solutions to all problems as being essentially technocratic in nature. Clearly, the computer age signifies a reverence for information. As Neil Postman (1984) observes:

The computer opened the age of information, but information for what and for whom? We are training our children to become information junkies, who believe that access to information is an end in itself. Thus the computer has essentially become a distracting technology because it encourages the mistaken belief that lack of information is an important problem, one which the machine will remedy. The computer makes it possible for children to have the same quantity of irrelevant information that adults have. (p. 78)

PARENTS AND THE COMMODIFICATION OF PLAY

The impetus behind the desire of parents to acquaint their children with computers is complex and rooted in the marketplace. In capitalist dominated economies there exists a powerful ethos of consumption. If consumption is the apogee of status, then personal productivity is an important medium through which it is reached.

In a highly competitive labor market with differential access to opportunities, only a select few will be in a position to fully enjoy the fruits of mobility and consumption. Most parents are painfully aware that economic opportunity is fast becoming a scarce commodity. Moreover, in the competitive marketplace the economic sin of "wasted time" is a mortal rather than venial one. Therefore, in a capitalist economy which underscores productive output, the play of children takes on a new meaning. Seeing one's child in "meaningless" and unstructured play appears, at least to the production and achievement oriented parent, as a waste of time of valuable time. In capitalism even child's play must furnish a commodity, or at least, lend itself to the future goal of production.

Playing on the innate fears and values of the achievement oriented parent, corporations have been successful in informing parents that for the child to meet to the future, he or she must accept and be familiar with the new technology. Computer exposure for the anxious parent represents a way to cut down on unproductive and wasteful play time, substituting instead, an early familiarity with the world of technology. Familiarizing children with computers, it is thought, increases their human capital and thereby gives them an edge in the workplace of the future. Children trained in the future skills necessary for production and consumption, become future producers in the making. While at one time we sacrificed young children to a life of desperate labor, we may now be sacrificing another generation of children to the process of preparing for labor. Both expropriate their childhood.

The usurpation and transformation of unstructured play time into producer related activities represents the commodification of play. As play becomes reified, and learning becomes a commodity designed soley to foster future economic mobility, the child's unstructured discovery of the world around them is sacrificed at the altar of market relations. The commodification of play robs the young child of a childhood unfettered by economic expectations, and hence cheats them out of a portion of their childhood. Capitalism thus enters the world of the child through the back door of their parents fears.

The commodification of play is rationalized by parents who believe they are helping the child to master the larger world. In pushing the child across the threshold of the technological future, parents may be creating a child who experiences the world not through their own eyes, but through the eyes of a software program designed by adults. These learning programs. supposedly based on the developmental perceptions of the child, are a phenomenological impossibility. Adults can never know the contours of the child's mind, as young children cannot understand the processes of the adult mind. What exists, then, are programs designed by adults based on what they believe to be the developmental and cognitive interests of children.

The world created by software programmers is a neat and predictable one. The linear relationship of cause and effect always prevail: when rules are followed the result is invariably the same. Unfortunately, human beings rarely live predictable, neat, cause-and-effect existences. To suggest to children—through the covert message incorporated in the technology—that life replicates technology is to deceive them.

Environments of cybernetic based information are limited by the binary capability of the technology, and the "grey" areas of existence—wisdom, compassion, and knowledge—can seldom be adequately addressed. The universe of software programs is the world of black-and-white. Computer technology is a perceptual domain where ambiguity is not tolerated, rote is the dominant mode, and moral questions must be begged. Although this system is efficient in transmitting bits of information, it cannot help children confront and answer the often painful moral and social questions that plague our society. Reliance on technological instruction may produce a student who is information rich, but it may also create a citizen who is morally impoverished. While information without compassion may be a desirable trait in machines, in human beings it is the mark of alienation.

PASSIVITY AND NON-CRITICAL ACCEPTANCE

Through the confinement of imagination characteristic of software boundaries, the perceived authority of the computer, the "absolute truth" that is supposedly a characteristic of information, and the absence of human dialogue, the child is aided in conforming to the world that is, rather than the world that should be. This scenario is exacerbated by the myth that information is value-free, a myth which presupposes that computers merely give information rather than information complemented by values. As the scenario suggests, computer technology may well encourage in the young a potential for social passivity and a non-critical perspective.

The potential for supporting a non-critical technocratic perspective is evident in the message of many of the current video games. While children have always played at war and destruction, video games reinforce more forcefully the child's disengagement from reality than do traditional games. Killing an enemy in video games entails "zapping" them with a shower of energy. Enemies merely disappear—there is no blood or bodies. The video game player is not killing humans, but unfamiliar things—aliens or spaceships. The "kill" is electronic: it is quick, hygienic, and one never faces the enemy head on. Concepts such as heroism and valor are absent from video games (as opposed to traditional games): what matters is the quantified kill—the number of dead enemies. All of this "killing" is done from an electronic distance and is short-lived; when it's over the enemy merely disappears from the screen. This new war game is juxtaposed to traditional games where bodies return to life, and acts of bravery are recognized.

It is no coincidence that the new war play emulates the new war mentality. Destruction in nuclear war occurs at a distance: the enemy is never seen (or is seen as blips on a screen), the destruction is not visible to the warrior (except, of course, the bodies on his or her side), and the whole battle is anonymous. Concepts such as heroism and bravery have no place in nuclear warfare.

Destruction oriented video games provide a testing ground for the future technological warrior. Children are taught to kill from a distance, to see their enemies as possessing no human characteristics, and to accept the "hygiene" of the kill. The fabric of video "kill games" contain no genuine feelings (Brod, 1984)—the player merely racks up points. Moreover, the sheer number of characters the player is able to kill is immense, thereby the huge amount of casualties that would be incurred in a nuclear war. Video games allow children to think of destruction in grand terms: the destruction of 500,000 aliens prepares children to imagine the destruction of hundreds of millions of human beings. This cool technocratic mode of thinking is a mandatory prerequisite for the nuclear warrior of the future. It is a short stem from "zapping" millions of enemies in a video game to annihilating millions of enemies in real life. Games replicate life.

The creation of the passive, technocratically obsessed, and alienated citizen of tomorrow, is a prime ingredient in a neo-Orwellian world of the future. While governments have always manipulated facts, the centrality of computer based information makes it a considerably easier task. The one who controls information controls imagination, and the one who controls imagination declares what is possible. Social choices have always been made based on what the body politic considers possible.

CONCLUSION

That we have entered the computer age is a far gone conclusion. Whatever current concern we have about technology is a moot point: computer technology is the reality of the present, and in all likelihood, it will be the dominant trend of the future. Moreover, authors do not wish to suggest a wholesale repudiation of computer technology is necessary. Computers have undeniably made life easier in many spheres, and in some operations, their efficiency is spectacular. We also do not maintain that children should be kept at a distance from computer technology. However, in a frenzied rush to introduce children to computer technology, the question of "why?" is often overlooked. Even though we have undeniably entered the computer age, is it necesary and desirable to introduce young children to computers? What are the possible negative consequences of encouraging early computer use?

In our rush to enter the world of microcomputers we often forget the power of the technology; especially its ability to change the users perceptions of space and time. Computers are not merely another gadget—they have the power to alter basic social relationships, and the power to shape social consciousness. In that sense, computers can either be a benefit to society or a curse. Or, put in another way, computers can either be a tool for liberation or an agent for repression.

References

Abt, C. (1980, March 12). What the computer holds for children in the T.V-computer age: Unprecedented promises and intolerable threats to child development. Paper presented at the National Council for Children, Families and the New Video/Computer Technologies, Princeton, N.J.

Barnes B. & Hill, S. (1983). Should your children work with microcomputers—logo before lego? *The Computing Teacher* **10**, 10-14.

Berger, Peter, & Luckman, T. (1967). *The social construction of reality: A treatise on the sociology of knowledge.* Garden City, N.J.: Doubleday Publishers.

Boulter, J. David. (1984). *Turing's man: Western culture in the computer age.* Chapel Hill: The University of North Carolina Press.

Brod, Craig, (1984). *Techno-stress.* New York: Addison Wesley.

Colker, Larry. (1983, October 14-15). Computers and play. Paper presented at the Conference for Young Child and the Computer: Building the Future Together, Columbus, OH.

Heller, R. & Martin C. (1982). *Bits and bits about computing: A computing literacy primer.* Rockville, MD: Computer Science Press.

Husserl, Edmond. (1931). *Ideas: general introduction to pure phenomenology.* New York: The MacMillan Co.

Klinzing, Dene G. (1985, March 31–April 4). A study of the behavior of children in a preschool equipped with computers. Paper presented at the Annual Meeting of the American Educational Research Association, 69th, Chicago, IL.

Postman, Neil. (1984, June). Quoted in Kid-friendly computers. *Parents,* **59**, 76-79.

Psathas, George. (1973). *Phenomenological sociology: issues and applications*. New York: John Wiley and Sons.

Seltzer, Michael & Karger, Howard. (1974, March). Good morning class, my name is bzzz vzzz crackle. *Ramparts*, **8**, 10-14.

Schneider, Mary F. & Schneider, Seymour. (1984, March). The computer age and family life. *Individual Psychology*, **40**, 61-70.

Schutz, Alfred. (1966). *Collected papers vol 1 and 2* Netherlands, The Hague: Martinus Nijhoff.

Sheingold, Karen. (1984). The microcomputer as a medium for young children. Technical Report No 26, Bank Street College of Education, New York, N.Y., Center for Children and Technology.

Spiegelberg, H. (1971). *The phenomenological movement*. Netherlands, The Hague: Martinus Nijhoff.

Williams, Ann R., & Beeson, B.S. (1985). The 'holding power' of the Computer: A study of young children's study time. University of Indiana, School of Education.

Wolff, Kurt. (1978). Phenomenology and sociology. In Bottomore, T. and Nisbet, R. (Eds). *A history of sociological analysis*. New York: Basic Books Inc.

CHAPTER 10

Computer Use With Young Children: Present Perspectives and Future Possibilities

PHILLIP B. WALDROP
Arkansas State University

Literature related to the use of computers with young children reveals a lack of objective information about the effects of the technology on learning. Much of the current information is based on subjective evaluations of personal experiences or on descriptive studies in which specific skills were taught through the use of computers. If significant contributions are to be made by the technology, a concerted effort must be made to objectively analyze the extant information and to focus on future investigations that might indicate those areas of the educational process most likely to benefit from technology. The purpose of this article is to provide an analysis of the current status of this approach in young child education and to present suggestions for future directions in research efforts.

KEY WORDS: Computer-assisted instruction, early childhood education.

IN RECENT years, an increasing amount of interest has been shown in integrating computer technology into the educational curriculum for young children. In reviewing the related literature, however, one is reminded why little true change occurs in educational practice. Much of the current thought in this area is based on the personal experiences of interested professionals, observation, limited demonstrations of various techniques and descriptive studies involving limited numbers of students.

Although many of the individuals who have successfully implemented some facet of computer technology with young children have called for research into the issue, very little true research has been done (Goodwin, Goodwin, Nansel, & Helm, 1986). As a result, much has been speculated as to the possible value of computers for young children, but little has been demonstrated in the way of the superiority (or lack of superiority) of this method over any other method.

If one draws on the experiences gained in other levels of education, some indication of future directions of computer use with young children may be gained. With older students, studies have suggested that computers show small, statistically significant advantages over other methods of instruction in accomplishing certain tasks (Kulik, Kulik, & Cohen, 1980; Kulik, Bangert, & Williams, 1983). Sufficient contradictory evidence exists in the current literature related to these older students, however, to suggest that the efficacy of the widespread use of computers in educational programs could be questioned. In this regard, the literature related to using computers with young children appears to be lagging slightly behind the other areas, but is proceeding along the same lines. That is, the initial claims are being challenged by objective analysis.

In the initial stages of the development of computer techniques in education, many individuals assumed that young children did not have a need for learning about or with computers. Further, questions were raised about the ability of the young child to perform any meaningful activity with a computer. With the advent of Papert's (1980) work, interest has been intensified in advancing young children's skills through the use of computers.

There are several factors, however, that may inhibit the development of computer use in education for young children. Goodwin, Goodwin, Nansel & Helm (1986) have indicated that problems identified in the literature include the lack of requisite skills in the children, the lack of quality software and the inadequate preparation of teachers. In addition, a large portion of the problem revolves around differences in motivations between those who advocate the innovation and those who resist.

Innovators, in their enthusiasm for the technique, see many applications and tend to engage in an ever extending search for new applications—that is, "what is possible." In pursuit of this goal, they often lose sight of "what is practical" in terms of uses that can be implemented by anyone in any classroom. In other words, the adequate resources of the research project do not always transfer to *all* situations. For example, methods for altering keyboards in various ways have been described (Hungate, 1982; Smithy-Willis, Riley, & Smith, 1982). Some of these methods require a certain degree of expertise on the part of the classroom teacher. In many cases, this expertise is not there.

An additional problem exists in that the questions being asked about the use of computers with young children are being asked by a group (adults) with, in large part, a mind set that may not be conducive to finding adequate answers. Cuffaro (1984) has cautioned against unthinkingly imposing an adult world concept on young children. There is a difference in orientation between adults who did not grow up with computers and young children who accept them as a normal part of everyday life. Some limitations that have been suggested by the intuition of adults have been demonstrated to not exist in reality with children.

These problems may be heightened by advocating immediate, broadly based infusion of the technology into the curriculum. Although the research basis for the use of computers with young children is limited, what evidence does exist suggests that solutions to these problems are available under the proper conditions. Before the technique joins similar past innovations in being relegated to the status of "educational fad," some attempt should be made to synthesize past efforts and to predict possible future areas for analysis. In obtaining a perspective, one might focus on two questions: 1) *Can* computers be used effectively to teach young children?; and 2) *Should* computers be used to teach young children?

EFFECTIVENESS OF COMPUTERS WITH YOUNG CHILDREN

As mentioned previously, much of the early resistance to the use of computers with young children focused on the presumed inability of the students to demonstrate the readiness skills necessary to successfully manipulate the computer. Advances in hardware have, to a large extent, rendered this point moot. Govier (1983) has described a special "concept keyboard" that makes use of touch pads on which the teacher can place overlays to use in a variety of drill and practice activities. Additional items include touch screens and voice input devices (Tan, 1985). In short, hardware is available to eliminate the early objections to the use of computers (Smithy-Willis, Riley, & Smith, 1982).

Assuming that the issue of hardware availability has been resolved (at least to the extent that expertise exists at the local level to use the hardware), the question remains of the financial ability of local districts to be able to avail themselves of the hardware. This issue is, however, beyond the realm of the present discussion. The effectiveness question raised here relates more to the ability of the computer to provide adequate experiences given its availability.

Although the literature does not support definitive answers to the question of whether or not computers are effective with young children, the information that exists would have to lead one to give at least a qualified "yes" to the question. The ultimate effectiveness is determined, as with all educational approaches, by the careful consideration of a variety of factors involved in successful use. Undoubtedly, the right hardware and software, used for an appropriate amount of time, with the appropriate type of student, by an appropriately trained teacher can produce a wide array of types of learning in young children. Most interest thus far has focused on teaching readiness skills, simple computer programming skills and socialization skills.

Effectiveness has been shown in using computers to teach reading readiness skills to children three and four years of age (Swigger and Campbell, 1981), skills from shape recognition to story building (Mander, 1982), visual discrimination (Smithy-Willis, Riley, & Smith, 1982), basic addition facts (Kraus, 1981), and spelling (Teague, Wilson & Teague, 1984). The problem with the existing evidence, however, is that very little has been done to indicate that computers can teach these and other skills better than other techniques (Ziajka, 1983).

In one study that *did* conduct direct comparisons, Goodwin, Goodwin, Nansel and Helm (1986) found that children who were taught prereading skills by computer performed no better on these cognitive tasks than did children who received no computer training. Additionally, students appeared to experience a *decrease* in interest in the computers after being exposed to them. This latter finding is at odds with most studies done with older students. This study had an acknowledged limitation in that the students were not exposed to the computer for an extended period of time. The discrepancy in outcomes among these studies again underscores the importance of considering a multiplicity of factors in determining effectiveness of teaching techniques.

As a second area of exploration, considerable interest has been created in the possibility of teaching higher level thinking skills to young children through the use of elementary computer programming. Bitter (1982) and Koetke (1984) have suggested that programming should be an integral part of integrating computers into the curriculum for young children. Others have questioned the ability of young children to perform the skills necessary for simple programming (Cuffaro, 1984).

Whether or not one accepts the premise that young children can program depends, in all likelihood, on the definition of programming that one is willing to accept. Ross and Campbell (1983) reported success in teaching first grade students in a Montessori classroom to do some programming in BASIC language. Most of the attention, however, has focused on the use of the LOGO language. Within this framework, definitions of programming tend to focus on the graphics capabilities of the language and on teaching the child to issue simple commands to produce certain figures and shapes.

Two notable examples indicate carefully structured programs that are based on responding to the needs and abilities of the young child. Campbell (1985) has developed a less difficult version of the LOGO language and described a sequence of activities leading to the end result of programming. This program, to a large extent, demonstrates the possibilities of involving the concrete experiences many feel are necessary prerequisites to the ability to engage in a complex task such as programming (Barnes & Hill, 1983; Duffaro, 1984). Clements (1983–1984) has also provided suggested language modifications to assist children in learning to effectively use LOGO. This approach focused on modifications in hardware and systematically graded steps in activities to lead the children into programming.

These studies would suggest that young children are capable of some rudimentary programming. The point of interest, however, involves the purpose in attempting to teach these skills. Reasons mentioned for teaching the skills include teaching the child to think, to engage in problem solving, to demonstrate competence and control over his/her environment, and to explore possible alternatives for action in the environment. Clements (1983–1984) indicated that students became more reflective and made fewer errors in assigned tasks, scored higher on tests of creative thinking, and were better at tasks involving discovering a missing step in a series of procedural rules in a game after completing his training program.

Hines (1983) concluded that all six children in her study learned to program (as she defined programming). When asked to perform specific tasks, however, the results were less striking. Two of the students could complete the task, two could partially complete the task, and one student could not complete the task. As stated earlier, one's definition of the tasks involved appears to say much about the efficacy of the approach. Clearly, as in other areas, much objective information remains to be generated.

A third area of interest involves the impact of computer use on the socialization skills of young children. Concern has been expressed that the nature of the activity will result in students sitting before the computer screen rather than engaging in social interaction with their peers (Cuffaro, 1984). Individuals who have used computers with young children, however, contend that new opportunities for socialization skills are presented (Waldrop, 1984; Tan, 1985; Ziajka, 1983). Clements (1983–1984) demonstrated one such opportunity in having students work in groups of three.

As a part of the discussion related to socialization possibilities, opinions have been presented by a number of individuals regarding the degree of adult involvement needed when children are working with computers. These opinions appear to be based on subjective observation in most cases. Goodwin, Goodwin, Nansel, and Helm (1986) compared the performance in skill acquisition of groups of children working with adult assistance and with minimal adult assistance. Their results indicated no significant differences in the skills gained by the groups.

In reviewing these attempts at demonstrating effectiveness of computers in the education of young children, one factor presents itself that may inhibit the utility to practitioners of the information generated. This is the lack of detailed descriptions of the conditions surrounding successful implementation of the techniques. It is this element that will make replication of the results possible. Further research that controls for this shortcoming has direct implications for the feasibility of implementing the available technology.

FEASIBILITY OF COMPUTER USE WITH YOUNG CHILDREN?

Most of the impetus for integrating computers into the curriculum for young children appears to come from adults who have, themselves, recently become interested in the tools. Avid proponents of the approach advocate immediate widescale implementation. Koetke (1984) cautions that public education will lose out in the technological push if computers are not used immediately. Mander (1982) posits that though other methods are used successfully to teach basic readiness skills, the fact that this is the computer age justifies widespread use.

Some individuals take a more moderate approach and urge cautious, thoughtful implementation (Cuffaro, 1984; Sprigle and Schaefer, 1984; Swigger and Campbell, 1981). Tan (1985) suggests implementation of the methodology as a supplement to, not as a replacement for, traditional instruction and concludes that mere contact with a computer is not sufficient reason for introducing computers into the curriculum. This would seem to be a reasonably approach since no evidence exists to indicate that there is any compelling reason for young children to use computers as a requisite for later life skills.

One philosophical position with considerable merit when arguing the issue within a societal context is a matter of equity of experience. An increasing number of children arrive at school having experience with computers in the home. The possibility exists that these children benefit from an advantage not available to everyone. Therefore, in order to remedy this discrepancy, it is perhaps necessary that schools must assume responsibility for ensuring that everyone has early, frequent exposure to the technology.

When attention is turned from a social/cultural debate, factors remain that are based on educational theory that have a bearing on feasibility decisions. For example, some concern has been expressed that the use of computers deprives young children of the concrete, three dimensional experience necessary for learning in the early years (Barnes & Hill, 1983; Cuffaro, 1984). In relating the technique to Piagetian principles, some individuals suggest that the child does not have the ability prior to about age seven (concrete operational stage) to get maximum usefulness from the computer (Burg, 1984; Cuffaro, 1984). Conversely, Prinz, Nelson, and Stedt (1982) have indicated that current research has called into question the limitations previously thought to exist in the ability of young children.

As stated previously, for all of the objections raised regarding the use of computers in educating young children, at least one study has been conducted to suggest that the objection is invalid. The overriding consideration at this point in determining the desirability of using the available technology appears to be the discovery of those conditions under which the computer can perform a specific educational task more efficiently, at less cost, than other techniques.

In the final analysis, no technique, in and of itself, has the capability to produce educational results. These results are brought about by the correct application of the appropriate material with the appropriate type of learner and by competent, enthusiastic teachers (Adams and Waldrop, 1985; Ziajka, 1983). In this vein, one must start with the educational goal and then fit the technique to the goal (Cuffaro, 1984; Waldrop, 1984). It is precisely this information that is not known about the use of computers with young children at this point.

Obviously, a considerable task lies ahead in determining those factors that *do* result in effective use. Specifically, a research agenda needs to be established in terms of effective uses of the available technology. The nature of the research must be of the true experimental type in which the use of computers is compared directly to other methods of instruction. The following items would appear to be essential to such an agenda:

1. *Identification of the requisite skills for effective computer use.* There is very little irrefutable evidence to suggest what skills are absolutely essential and the age at which those skills could reasonably expected to be manifested.

2. *Identification of results that can be expected with computer use with a wide variety of learning styles.* Many of the studies that have been done to this point report success in using the computer to attain results in cognitive and social domains. In certain cases, these studies have ignored the differential effects among students.

3. *Identification of the impact of various student factors in the results obtained.* Based on existing research, this list would surely include, but not be limited to, sex, general academic ability, age, time involved in instruction, variations in demonstrated academic achievement.

4. *Identification of the hardware/software design features that enhance effectiveness.* A large amount of information has been provided to suggest what these features are based on experience. Evidence needs to be acculumated to identify essential features.

5. *Identification of the extent to which skills learned through the use of computers transfer to other areas and factors which affect transfer.* Without the transfer of skills from one situation to another, one must question the goals of any particular educational technique. This one is certainly no exception.

6. *Identification of the knowledge and skills needed by teachers to effectively use computers with young children.* As stated earlier, many of the strategies that have been used to produce learning through computer use have

suggested the need for a fairly sophisticated practitioner to be available. Determination needs to be made of the skills needed by various school personnel to effectively implement the technology. Additionally, identification of effective strategies for training inservice and preservice personnel in these skills is necessary.

Certainly this does not comprise an exhaustive list of the questions remaining to be answered. Regardless of the sense of urgency that derives from fear of depriving young children of a necessary skill for survival in the information age, unjudicious application of educational techniques/materials in the past has led to the demise of more than one promising approach. With the preceding considerations as a basis, this particular approach carries the promise of many opportunities for genuine advancement of educational practice.

References

Adams, T., & Waldrop, P. (1985). Computer-assisted instruction in teacher education. *The Physical Educator*, **43**(3), 156–160.

Barnes, B., & Hill, S. (1983). Should young children work with microcomputers— LOGO before LEGO? *The Computing Teacher*, **10**(9), 11–14.

Bitter, G. (1982). The road to computer literacy. Part II: Objectives and activities for grades K-3. *Electronic Learning*, **2**(2), 34–37, 85–86.

Campbell, S. (1985). Preschoolers meet a high tech turtle. *Science and Children*, **22**(7), 37–40.

Clements, D. (1983–1984). Supporting your young children's LOGO programming. *The Computing Teacher*, **11**(5), 24–30.

Cuffaro, H. (1984). Microcomputers in education: Why is earlier better? *Teachers College Record*, **85**(4), 560–569.

Goodwin, L., Goodwin, W., Nansel, A., & Helm, C. (1986). Cognitive and affective effects of various types of microcomputer use by preschoolers. *American Educational Research Journal*, **23**(3), 348–356.

Govier, H. (1983). Keyboards made simple. *Child Education*, October, 16–17.

Hines, S. (1983). Preschoolers computers = ABC: Computer programming abilities of five year old children. *Educational Computer*, **3**(4), 10–12.

Hungate, H. (1982). Computers in the Kindergarten. *The Computing Teacher*, **9**(5), 15–18.

Hunter, B. (1981–1982). Computer literacy in grades K-8. *Journal of Educational Technology Systems*, **10**, 59–66.

Koetke, W. (1984). Computers, children and learning: One complete iteration. *Creative Computing*, **10**(11), 163–164, 169.

Kraus, W. (1981). Using a computer game to reinforce skills in addition basic facts in second grade. *Journal for Research in Mathematics*, **12**(March), 152–155.

Kulik, J., Kulik, C., & Cohen, P. (1980). Effectiveness of computer-based college teaching: A meta-analysis of findings. *Review of Educational Research*, **50**(4), 525–544.

Kulik, J., Bangert, R., & Williams, G. (1983). Effects of computer-based teaching on secondary school students. *Journal of Educational Psychology*, **75**(1), 19–26.

Mander, C. (1982). An Oakville enterprise: Computers teach preschoolers to read and write. *Canadian Library Journal*, **39**(February), 17–18.

Papert, S. (1980). *Mindstorms: Children, computers, and powerful ideas.* New York: Basic Books.

Prinz, P., Nelson, K., & Stedt, J. (1982). Early reading in young deaf children using microcomputer technology. *American Annals of the Deaf*, **127**, 529–535.

Ross, S., & Campbell, L. (1983). Computer-based education in the Montessori classroom: A compatible mixture? *Technological Horizons in Education Journal*, **11**, 105–109.

Smithy-Willis, D., Riley, M., & Smith, D. (1982). Visual discrimination and preschoolers. *Educational Computer Magazine*, **2**(6), 19, 45.

Sprigle, J., & Schaefer, L. (1984). Age, gender, and spatial knowledge influence on preschoolers' computer programming abilities. *Early Child Development and Care*, **14**(3–4), 243–250.

Swigger, K., & Campbell, J. (1981). The computer goes to nursery school. *Educational Computer Magazine*, **1**(2), 10–12.

Tan, L. (1985). Computers in preschool education. *Early Child Development and Care*, **19**(4), 319–336.

Teague, G., Wilson, R., & Teague, M. (1984). Use of computer assisted instruction to improve spelling proficiency of low achieving first graders. *AEDS Journal*, **17**(4), 30–35.

Waldrop, P. B. (1984). Behavior reinforcement strategies in computer-assisted instruction: Programming for success. *Educational Technology*, **24**(9), 38–41.

Ziajka, A. (1983). Microcomputers in early childhood education? A first look. *Young Children*, **38**(5), 61–67.

CHAPTER 11

The Technological World-View and The Responsible use of Computers in the Classroom*

JOHN W. MURPHY
University of Miami
and
JOHN T. PARDECK
Southeast Missouri State University

In this paper it is argued that technology does not merely represent a set of devices that teachers may choose to use, but more importantly advances a world-view that shapes social existence. The image of social life that technology conveys are not currently receiving serious consideration from those who are rushing head-long to incorporate computers into the classroom. As a result, the possible deletirious consequences of a technological education are not being exposed. This paper attempts to correct this deficiency by addressing the philosophy of technology and its impact on education.

PRESENTLY technology is proliferating throughout the United States at an unprecedented rate. In particular, the computer has made its way into the home, farm, and factory, not to mention the classroom. Great claims are made by those who favor this increase in computerization, as this particular form of technology is thought to be capable of solving many of our social problems. However, the introduction of this technology into the classroom may have adverse effects which can be anticipated and possibly diverted, yet will most likely be overlooked until the problems surface. This is the case for the following reason: the philosophical world-view which accompanies technology, the images of the classroom, learning, and students which are advanced by technological rationality may go undetected.

Therefore, the aim of this paper is to detail the philosophical principles of modern technology so that its raison d'etre is revealed. Specially, we argue that technology portrays social existence quite

---

* Journal of Education, Volume 167, Number 2, 1985 © Trustees of Boston University.

negatively, and may actually stifle the critical and creative style of learning that most educators extol. Moreover, this not simply a matter of careless pedagogical procedures, but, more importantly, stems from philosophical principles that underlie modern technology. Mere technological changes designed to humanize the use of computers by educators may exacerbate, instead of ameliorate, an unpleasant situation in the classroom.

THE TECHNOLOGICAL WORLD-VIEW

The central difficulty with technology is that is denies the "life-world" from which it originates. As Merleau-Ponty (1964a) states, the life-world (*Lebenswelt*) is the domain filled by "living history and the spoken word", and therefore is the source of all social meaning. Specifically, the life-world is the living presence to which all persons adhere prior to Cartesian distinctions — that is, the world inscribed by human *praxis* (Merleau-Ponty, 1964b). This living world, as Schutz and Luckmann (1973) state, embodies the "meaning-strata which transforms natural things into cultural objects, human bodies into fellow-men, and the movements of fellow-men into acts, gestures, and communication" (p. 5).

Of key importance is that the world is not objective in the Cartesian sense, but exists *for someone*. All knowledge, stated simply, is mediated by the constitutive activity of human experience, and thus represents neither crudely realistic events nor a Kantian "in-itself". The world's meaning is a social product, as human action is at the heart of all phenomena.

As should be immediately noted, when the world is envisioned to be a life-world the significance of human action cannot be diminished, as in theories which maintain that phenomena have a self-same, or objective identity, immune to the influence of human intentions. When conceived objectively, a phenomenon's identity is not incumbent upon human action, and subsequently individuals are unable to treat it creatively. Yet it is precisely this creative tendency that technology aims to suppress.

What are the central tenets of the technological world-view? Modern writers have described them as follows (Lenk, 1973): First, technology materializes existence, as the world is conceived to be matter, pure extension, and thus an objective thing. Second, mathematics is the language of technology, which means that a rational calculus is employed to conceptualize the world. Third, the logic of matter is assumed to govern individual behavior and social order. And fourth, both individuals and society are portrayed as part of an objective order which is thoroughly asocial.

As a consequence of these traits, Ihde (1979) declares that technology offers a style of social imagery which he calls "instrumental realism". Technology, he suggests, establishes its own form of reason for assessing the world. This technological rationality, as it is sometimes called, is typically, thought to represent the paragon of reason, because it is ostensibly divorced from the passion indigenous to human action. Because this modality of reason is assumed to represent objective standards it claims to furnish the most reliable method available for making judgments. Technology, in this sense, defines the world in such a way that a precise and persistent relationship is established among its parts. As Mumford (1963) remarks, this allows phenomena to be controlled in a manner which is impossible when the so-called human element is not checked. With the human side of life rendered ancillary to technical reason, technology becomes an impregnable force. It is in this respect that Ellul (1964) refers to persons as enslaved to modern technology, as its logic becomes synonymous with reason.

When technological thinking comes to dominate the social scene, certain problems begin to appear. Particularly significant is that human cognition, action, and learning begin to assume a technological hue. Human existence becomes technologized, thereby creating the illusion that technology is autonomous or essentially unrelated to the contingencies which are presumed to be indigenous to human action. Because technology instills reason where it is presumed to be missing, humans by definition are enslaved by this rationality.

Accordingly, Heidegger (1967, pp. 14–15) says that technology "sets upon nature" and "makes 'unreasonable demand(s)' on both nature and man". Technology can do this, he contends, because it is not treated as a modality of human existence. Technology established itself as what Marcuse (1964) calls a "veil" that separates human action from the world; or, as Habermas (1978) states, it advances principles that demand universal recognition, and therefore has a status identical to "ideology". Stated simply, technology, "deanimates" social life, as it displaces human action by inserting its own form of rationality at the center of existence (Ihde, 1982). This does not mean, some critics suggest, that individuals are dehumanized by technology merely because they must work with machines, but more importantly because the logic of technology is assumed to be objective, ahistorical, and thus, undaunted by existential contingencies (Caldwell, 1981).

What this means is that a functional image of social existence is promoted, as exemplified by the work of Talcott Parsons. According to his technological or cybernetic rendition of the social world, the only knowledge that can unite society exists objectively. Consequently, individuals must imagine themselves to be subordinate to the source of order and adjust to its demands, since they are only able to supply the energy required to enliven the social system and cannot give it direction (Parsons, 1966).

When the world is conceived in this way, the "history of transcendental consciousness (is) no more than the residue of the history of technology" (Habermas, 1971). Since human action merely supports an imperious technological system, behavior is considered worthwhile only when this function is adequately performed. Stated otherwise, the goal of human action is the maintenance of the social system and not liberation or self-determination. Marcuse (1964) argues that this results in persons living in a "one-dimensional" world, where only the dominant values and norms are treated as legitimate and all opposition to them is eviscerated. Therefore, the only behaviour that is evaluated positively is that which acquiesces to authority and unquestioningly adopts traditional ways of acting.

In short, the obfuscation of the life-world culminates in an externalized locus of social order and belief that persons are living in a society that exists *sui generis*. Usually this is referred to as social ontological realism, as the system is the only thing that is considered to be real and everything else is assumed to be derived from it. This image of existence requires that the social system be understood to supply individuals with their identity, and therefore they are forever indebted to this source for their meaning (Stark, 1963).

Both Marxists and functionalists, in contending that education serves to sustain the status quo, generally suggest that this process is overtly coercive and manipulative. The world-view advanced by technology, however, may unobstrusively promote an identical policy. Thus, both radicals and conservatives may want to take note of how technology accomplishes this ignoble feat.

TECHNOLOGY AND LEARNING

Atomization. Technology tends to atomize or fragment the learning process, thus resulting in what Sartre (1977) calls "serialization". Because persons must adjust themselves to a mechanical learning device, closely monitor its instructions, follow its commands, and supply appropriate responses at the right time, a state of isomorphism is reached whereby a student's intentions are subsumed by the directives that are issued. This means that the learning process is ahistorical, since an inanimate object establishes the framework (*Lebensraum*) for all learning.

Accordingly, as Straus (1963) writes, no "play space" is present between an instrument's instructions and a student's repsonse, but instead all choices are made ex post facto, or after they are legitimized by a machine and cognitively imprinted. This results in a style of technological "forced feeding". And when learning is understood in this manner, the dynamism that is possible in a classroom can never be realized. For example, knowledge cannot be challenged, expanded, and its symbolic nature revealed, as when information is bandied about in a classroom. Particularly, students may miss the importance of interpretation in acquiring knowledge and the role this activity plays in shaping society. For as Sartre (1977) points out, when learning is serialized then brute matter, as opposed to *praxis,* mediates human relations, leaving persons alone to face what seems to be an intractable reality.

Monological discourse. Technological learning relies on discourse that is thoroughly monological. Communication is monological when it

> attributes the intersubjectivity of meaning, that is the mutual sharing of identical meanings to the fact that sender and receiver — each an entity for itself — are previously equipped with the same program. (Habermas, 1970, p. 131)

Because information proceeds from a single sender to a receiver without the meaning of these transmissions being questioned, everyone is assumed to operate according to universal (ahistorical) principles of logic, rationality, and speech. To use Perelman's (1979) well-known phrase, technological education treats students as if they are members of a "universal audience" and use an identical cognitive style.

Technological pedagogy epitomizes monological discourse. For instance, information is presented by an agent which is not susceptable to critique or interrogation, and thus knowledge can only be recorded and not actively analyzed. Additionally, all transmissions are structured according to the requirements of Aristotelian logic, as all answers to questions are presented as binary alternatives. Although this method of communication eliminates ambiguity from the process of identifying a correct answer, the need for persons to learn how to classify and generalize — in other words to think — is systematically reduced. A priori categories are merely mastered, and date placed into them, without students understanding how or why a particular classificatory scheme is used. Consequently, students are unable to cope with situation where the standard cognitive categories do not apply. They have not learned how to improvise, or *interpret* information in an effective manner, as this requires an active mind.

Instrumental learning. Technology promotes what Horkheimer (1974) calls "instrumental learning". The general aims of computerized learning are to process information rapidly, identify relationships, and reduce a person's response time. Although information passes before one's eyes quickly, as in video games and speed reading, little else is accomplished. All that is fostered is a type of "means-end" rationality, whereby students learn to follow premises to their logical conclusions as expeditiously as possible. Accordingly, it is assumed that a single system of logic underpins all rational thinking, and that educated persons must know its laws. Quickness of response is considered to be a valid index for measuring learning, as efficiency and accuracy are thought to be at the heart of intelligent behavior. Gifted persons, moreover, are believed to be able to master the principles of reason faster than those who are less talented.

Clearly, this style of cognition is advantageous in a modern bureaucratic society like our own (Weber, 1947). A bureaucratic society is characterized by increasing rationality, as rules become more formal and legalisatic and social and political distinctions become more detailed. If persons are to function adequately, cognitive complexity must be fostered, yet there are drawbacks to this type of thinking. Most important, learning in this system is discursive and not critical, primarily because the discovery of detail is given the highest priority. This results in mental acuity and not inventiveness, since the mind is not trained to transcend the data that are presented. And without this ability, critical insight, imagination, and creativity are impossible.

Inhibiting of inquiry. When knowledge is conveyed technologically it is presented as a set of fully developed "either/or" options that are understood through repetition. Learning is assumed to have occurred when students are able to apply this logic to concrete situations through problem-solving exercises. As a result, learning is made relevant because knowledge is put into practice. Nevertheless, this type of knowledge application may in fact inhibit regions inquiry.

This is the case for the following reasons. First, practice is solely a matter of reiteration and not reflection. Thus, knowledge is adopted and implemented without being thoroughly scrutinized. Second, personal or pragmatic motives do not determine the utility of knowledge. Instead, information is valued because of its clarity, reproducibility, and immediate social utility, as opposed to its thought-provoking character. And third, because the logic that is indigenous to technology is not subject to question, social existence is portrayed abstractly throughout the learning process. This results in reductionism, since any particular rendition of "reality" is given credence only if it conforms to the strictures imposed by technological rationality (Horkheimer, 1982). Therefore, life is dominated and rationalized by a specific logic, while social existence is explained but not necessarily understood. As a consequence of this approach to learning students are taught, not to investigate a situation, but to apply ready-made axioms that may seriously distort the actual intentions of persons. Clearly, this is a poor substitute for investigative integrity.

The marginalization of morality. And finally, technological pedagogy offers an image of social order that is amoral (Apel, 1979), because technology portrays social life as if it were objective and consisted of a fixed set of behavioral and congnitive options. The purpose of education, accordingly, is to acquaint students with these norms so that they become socially competent. Although it is certainly not the aim of educators to curtail divergent thinking through their use of technology, independent thought is not fostered when information is divorced from human action. If persons are not conceived to be self-directed and able to recognize themselves in their actions, the idea of social morality cannot be sustained (Dewey, 1916). Apel (1979) explains how morality is eliminated as a consequence of technology reducing the significance of interpretation.

Because technology "rationalizes" learning, thereby eliminating *interpretation* from education, social fragmentation is promoted. This happens because knowledge is not viewed to be a collective product but rather is assumed to be individually generated. Because technology does not allow knowledge acquisition to be a "purposive-rational activity", a matter of decision and interpretation, one person alone, involved in a "subject-object" relationship to facts, is believed to be able to discover truth (Apel, 1979). However, when learning is understood to be a thoroughly interpretive activity, and not merely based on perceptual or logical precision, the issue of intersubjective validity is raised. That is, interpretation presupposes the existence of a variety of interpretations, a community of interpreters, the need to recognize all interpretations, since none by definition is absolute. A procedure for merging these interpretations into a common body of knowledge is required. In short, interpretive learning recognizes both self and other as central to obtaining knowledge, as opposed to treating education as an asocial process which stresses the collection of facts.

THE RESPONSIBLE USE OF TECHNOLOGY

As might be expected, the plans that are usually proposed to humanize the use of educational technology are preponderately structural (Bjorn-Anderson & Rasmussen, 1980). Attention has been directed to redesigning classrooms in order to integrate technology smoothly into the everyday affairs of both students and faculty members. For example, it has been suggested that curriculum and environmental fragmentation can be corrected by transforming traditional classrooms into seminar rooms or laboratories which facilitate interaction among students and teachers (Kurland, 1968). Some planners argue that opportunities should be provided regularly for students to share their ideas, while they each pursue their own particular program of learning (Brabner, 1970). Most recently this issue of humanizing technology has been raised in terms of establishing an appropriate interface between computers and humans, mostly a logistic undertaking aimed at enabling students to "talk" effectively with computers (Goldes, 1983).

For the most part, these strategies treat technology as a tool that can be humanized if its rules of operation are mastered. What has to be done, accordingly, is to create a setting in which this information can be disseminated to all users. Once a proper environment is furnished, educators assume that a commodious relationship will flourish between technology and those who use it. What this scenario over-looks, however, is that technology *is not a tool* which can be assimilated readily into the classroom by altering environmental conditions. Technology is not passive, but instead promulgates a world-view which shapes a society's identity. In fact, persons may begin to define themselves and their culture technologically, and when this occurs the usual structural approaches to humanizing technology are ineffective.

Inevitably, an autonomous technology which reduces the importance of human action in learning will severely disrupt and limit the learning process. This is not to say that educators must abandon the use of technological rationality from appearing to be autonomous and the nemesis of *praxis*. Technology, in other words, must be reintegrated into the human condition and not simply assimilated into the environment of a classroom.

Most important when establishing this new ground for technology is to recognize that the world is neither subjective nor objective, but subtends this Cartesian differentiation. Technological rationality employs the Cartesian distinction and thus projects an image of an objective world that is allowed to control individual behaviour. Yet if technology is ever to be responsible to its creators it cannot be perceived as immune to existential claims. Therefore, technology must also be understood to emanate from what Merleau-Ponty (1968) calls the "Chiasm", the intertwining of objectivity and subjectivity that is central to human action. Education must no longer be oriented in terms of those ancient maxims which claim to provide access to ideal or timeless truth. People must not be "led out" of the world as a result of their education, but only out of darkness. In other words, education should return persons to the world, as opposed to starting them on a journey which culminates in them denying their existence.

This world, however, it not the mundane world which students must try to mollify. Rather, this is the world of direct experience, an existential claim, which is the only type of world that individuals can call their own. The world that educators must resurrect, stated simply, is the "lived-world", the pre-objective world that is sustained by human *praxis*. Education must be understood to be an interpretive process which emphasizes the mystery of inquiry instead of the acquisition of fixed principles. Most important is that technology is implicated in the opacity of the lived-world, and accordingly cannot claim to have a seignorial status above the melange of truths that compete for dominance in everyday life.

When understood as autonomous, technology can only provide one interpretation of knowledge, specifically the rendition which is consistent with its world-view. But when technology is understood to emerge from the lived-world, its image is distinctly altered. It can no longer be viewed as an autonomous entity than can justifiably shape human actions. Human action, instead, sustains technology, and consequently, technological rationality represents merely another modality of *praxis*, not the ultimate measure of knowledge. Subtending the technological world-view is the human ability to challenge any picture of reality presented; therefore, technology cannot legitimately claim to dictate knowledge.

If we make this theoretical shift, technology assumes what Marcuse (1978) refers to as an "aesthetic" identity. Technology does not supply its own parameters for identifying information; rather, it rests on a base of human action and owes its significance or meaning to this expressive human dimension. With this aesthetic backdrop, technology's attempt to deanimate social existence is sharply curtailed. Only then can technology be used critically, as a facilitator of human imagination, rather than assuming control of learning.

SOCRATIC QUESTIONS IN THE HIGH-TECH AGE

Merely adding more technology to an already abstract teaching strategy will not make education more socially responsible. In order to foster the humanization of technology, questions that pertain to the human ground of technology must be addressed. The issues that have always concerned educators are not technological, but those of lived existence, such as the meaning of life, the nature of social relationships, commitment, the need for community, and the value of ethical behavior (Weizenbaum, 1976).

In fact, philosophers have characteristically argued that discussions about these aspects of life have saved humans from barbarism. Although technological rationality may be important in shaping the modern view of pedagogy, these Socratic issues remain at the heart of education. Education, therefore, can never be concerned solely with the acquisition of techniques, because technology is sustained by principles which are much more fundamental than technological rationality. Accordingly, educators must never abdicate their responsibility to raise more than technical questions in the classroom, even though the technological ethic may devalue this type of study.

This shift toward understanding technology to be a social form of reasoning has significant implications for educational policy. First, humanizing technology should not be limited to making logistical adjustments to its presence in the classroom. Second, technology should not be discussed merely in terms of mastering techniques, but more importantly its relationship to human destiny. Third, the implementation of technology must be understood as replete with social, ethical, and political consequences, in addition to technical difficulties. And fourth, technology should not be allowed to overshadow the Socratic questions which pertain to self-knowledge, as often occurs when persons are enamored of the application of technological rationality.

Anyone who has worked with students recently will recognize that these recommendations pose a significant challenge to educators. Students seem to find the ethical, political, and social implications of technology bothersome, as they want to move ahead undaunted with its application. Many programs have been inaugurated which attempt to combine technological training with the arts, so as to provide students with an enlightened perspective on technology. Yet for the most part they have been unsuccessful, primarily because technology is thought to be scientific and convey truth, while the arts offer opinion. Before the humanization of technology can be taken seriously its world-view must be exposed, as this philosophy is cajoling persons into indifference about their humanity. In this way, technology will be placed in the service of humanity and humanized. It must be remembered that without this philosophical shift technology can never be brought under human control. And as should be noted, merely adding more technology to an already abstract teaching strategy will not make technological education socially responsible. Educators must understand that if the world-view of technology is not examined seriously, technological rationality may promote apathy on the part of students by encouraging them to take a nonreflective attitude toward society. And because this conception of education is unconscionable to most teachers, we must take care not to foster inadvertently this style of learning through our use of technology in the classroom.

References

Apel, K-O. (1979). The common presuppositions of hermeneutics and ethics: Types of rationality beyond science and technology. In J. Sallis (Ed.), *Studies in phenomenology and the human sciences* (pp. 35–55). Atlantic Highlands, NJ: Humanities Press.

Ballard, E.G. (1981). Man or technology: Which is to rule? In S. Skousgaard (Ed.), *Phenomenology and the understanding of human destiny* (pp. 3–19). Washington DC: University Press of America.

Bjorn-Anderson, N., & Rasmussen, L.B. (1980). Sociological implications of computer systems. In H.T. Smith and T.R. Green (Eds.), *Human interaction with computers* (pp. 57–123). London: Academic Press.

Brabner, G. (1970). The decline of pedagocentricity. *Educational Technology*, **10**(11), 11–18.

Caldwell, R. (1981). Computers and curriculum promises and problems. In Institute for Educational Leadership (Ed.), *Technology and education* (pp. 257–270).

Dewey, J. (1916). *Democracy and education.* New York: Macmillan.

Ellul, J. (1964). *The technological society.* New York: Random House.

Goldes, H.J. (1983). Designing the human-computer interface. *Educational Technology*, **23**(10), 9–15.

Habermas, J. (1970). Toward a theory of communicative competence. In H.P. Dreitzel (Ed.), *Recent sociology No. 2* (pp. 114–148). New York: Macmillan.

Habermas, J. (1971). *Knowledge and human interests.* Boston: Beacon Press

Habermas, J. (1978). Problems of legitimation in late capitalism. In P. Connerton (Ed.), *Critical sociology* (pp. 363–387). New York: Penguin Books.

Heidegger, M. (1967). *Vortrage und Aufsatze* [Lectures and Essays], Teil l. Pfulligen: Verlag Gunther Neske.

Horkheimer, M. (1974). *Critique of instrumental reason.* New York: Seabury Press.

Horkheimer, M. (1982). *Critical theory.* New York: Continuum Publishing.

Ihde, D. (1979). *Technics and praxis.* Dordrecht: D. Reidel.

Ihde, D. (1982). *The historical-ontological priority of technology over science.* Paper presented at the International Conference on Philosophy and Science in Phenomenological Perspective, Buffalo, NY.

Kurland, N.D. (1968). The impact of technology on education. *Educational technology* 8, (20), 12–15.

Lenk, H. (1973). *Technokratie als ideologie* [Technocracy as Ideology]. Stuttgart: Verlag W. Kohhammer.

Marcuse, H. (1964). *One-dimensional man.* Boston: Beacon Press.

Marcuse, H. (1968). *The aesthetic dimension.* Boston: Press.

Merleau-Ponty, M. (1968). *The visible and the invisible.* Evanston: Northwestern University Press.

Mumford, L. (1963). *Technics and civilization.* New York: Harcourt, Brace and World.

Parsons, T. (1966). *Societies: Evolutionary and comparative.* Englewood Cliffs, NJ: Prentice-Hall.

Perelman, C. (1979). *The new rhetoric and humanities.* Dordrecht: D. Reidel.

Sartre, J.P. (1977) *Life/situations.* New York: Pantheon Books.

Schutz, A., & Luckmann, T. (1973) *The structures of the life-world.* Evanston: Northwestern University Press.

Stark, W. (1963). *The fundamental forms of social thought.* New York: Fordham
    University Press.
Straus, E. (1963). *The primary world of the senses.* New York: The Free Press.
Weber, M. (1947). *Social and economic organization.* New York: Macmillan.
Weizenbaum, J. (1976). *Computer power and human reason.* New York: W.H. Freeman.

Index

Aids, computer   2
Artificial intelligence   4, 5
Assessment, in competence of skill
   acquisition   86–88

Berger, Peter   108
Binary system   100

CALIP (Computer Aptitude, Literacy,
   Interest Profile)   30
Child-centered learning
   computer programming in LOGO   3, 4
   mathematics   3
   word processing   2
Cognition   3, 13, 100
Cognitive developments,
   see Piaget, Jean
Cognitivism   3
Colby, Kenneth   9
Commonsense knowledge,
   artificial intelligence and   4
Competence
   computer programming and   58
   stage of skill acquisition   58
Computer age, literacy needed for
   2, 114, 131
Computer-assisted instruction (CAI)
   limitations of   54
   See also Tutor, computer as
Computer culture   98
Computer games   72, 117
Computer literacy
   appeal of, as ideology   47–48
   arguments for   48
   control surrendered by   48
   employment   48–51
   political socialization of the child
      104, 140–141
   student   48

Concrete operational level, computer
   used at   12
Concrete operations, Piaget on   12
Control
   computer literacy   12–14
   shared by child with microcomputer
      11–14, 72–74
CPAB (Computer Programmer
   Aptitude Battery)   29
Creativity, computer and   5, 104
CSAB (Comprehensive Skills
   Assessment Battery)   86
Cuffaro, Harriet   2, 23, 125
Curriculum, computer programming
   43, 121–123

DAISEY (Developmental Assessment
   and Instruction for Success in
   Early Years)   8, 85–90
Destruction of education, computer
   causing   6, 97–105, 131–140
Developmental stages,
   see Piaget, Jean
Dewey, John 137
DIAL-R (Developmental Indicator
   for the Assessment of Learning-
   Revised)   7, 77
Differences, use of microcomputers to
   teach in early childhood   11–14
Disabilities, microcomputer used for
   children   2
Dreyfus, Herbert and Stuart   4, 102
Drill, computer for   3, 13

Early childhood education, use of
   microcomputer in   11–14, 123–128
   See also Piaget, Jean
Education
   computer literacy stress   45–48

technology of computers controlling
98–100
Educational aids, computers as   2
Educational software   2
Educational technology,
see Technology
Ellul, Jacques   97
Epistemological theory   3
Eye-hand coordination, use of
microcomputer to teach in early
childhood   24

Graphics, on computer   24
Guattari, Félix   101

Habermas, Jürgen   133, 134
Hardware   5, 124
Hunter, Beverly   48

Idealism, computer literacy and   48
Ideology, computer literacy as   100–102
Instrumental learning   136
Invisible pedagogy, of computerized
curriculum   100–102, 141

Jobs, computer literacy for   48–51

Lebenswelt   8, 132
Logic, computer weakening in child   5–6
LOGO   3, 4
Luehrman, Arthur   48

Mathematics, computer and LOGO   3
Merton, Robert   103
Microcomputers, issues   1
Microworld
acquisition   9, 11–14
advanced-beginner stage of skill
9, 11–14
Minsky, Marvin   98
Moursund, David   49

Neo-Orwellian world   118
Novice
computers   11–14
stage of skill acquisition   12

Papert, Seymour   3, 13, 122
Parsons, Talcott   134
Person-machine interaction   3
Phenomenology   107

Piaget, Jean
cognitive structures and   3, 13
computer and   3
concrete operations   12
LOGO and   3
Preoperational stage   6
Practice, computer   9, 11–14
Praxis   139, 140
Preschool, microcomputers   13
Process, use of microcomputer to teach
in early childhood   11–14, 123–128
Proficiency
computer programming and
63, 125
failure   124
stage of skill acquisition   11–14
programmed instruction   11–14
texts for   68
Programming
curriculum determined by   121-123
technological threat to education
48, 108–110
See also LOGO, Papert, Seymour,
Tutee, computer as

Rules   125

Sartre, Jean Paul   135
Schank, Roger   5
Scoring, computers   77–83
Simmon, Herbert   4
Simulators, computers as   128
Skill acquisition
advanced beginner   11–14
competence   11–14
computer as tutee and   2
computer as tutor and   2
novice   9, 11–14
Skill-oriented activities, use of
microcomputer to teach in early
childhood   11–14, 63–68
Software   22, 24–25, 83

Taylor, Robert   2
Teachers
expert   1
improving effectiveness of   1, 3
Technical devices, computers used
as   2
Technological progress, education as
means to end of   45–48

Technological "World-View"   98, 131, 134
Technology
    computer literacy and support for   45
    value of, in education   45–46
Thinking
    computer and thinking about   98
    role of image   98
Timing, use of microcomputer to develop in early childhood   11–14, 123–128
Tool, computer as   2, 139
Turtle geometry
    computer and   17
    See also LOGO
Tutee, computer as   2
    limitations of   3
    See also Programming
Tutor, computer as   2
    limitations   3

Value-free   98
Value neutrality, of computer   117
Violence, microcomputer leading to   114, 118

Weber, Max   108, 136
Weizenbaum, Joseph   100, 140
Wilensky, Robert   4
Winograd, Terry   5
Word processing   2